Creative Learning for Inclusion

Creative Learning for Inclusion explores the crucial role that creativity can play in inclusive education. It outlines a number of practical challenges faced by teachers working in both mainstream and special schools and the conceptual issues which frame successful learning for young people with special needs. It shows teachers practical examples of how to use creativity in the curriculum, and also how to engage with and support the learning of pupils with special educational needs in a way that will substantially impact their school experiences and later lives.

This book collects together six accounts of creative approaches to meet special needs. These case studies are written by teachers and creative practitioners, each one considering a different theme:

- the importance of location and context
- early years
- sustainability of practice
- the assessment of learning
- creative uses of technology
- student participation.

Describing the different ways in which a creative approach can help pupils with SEN access the curriculum, with activities and practical materials for teachers, this book will explain:

- why creativity is central to making the curriculum accessible
- how to use personalised learning with pupils with SEN
- how to promote achievements and motivation through creative experiences
- how the curriculum can be extended and represented in innovative ways for pupils with SEN
- how to use interactive methods of teaching and alternative methods of communication.

Creative Learning for Inclusion is an invaluable guide for all those involved in teaching and engaging young people with special needs.

Edward Sellman is a Lecturer in Special Needs at the University of Nottingham, UK

Creative Teaching/Creative Schools Series

Series Editors: Pat Thomson, Julian Sefton-Green and Naranee Ruthra-Rajan

Leading a Creative School: Initiating and Sustaining School Change
Ethel Sanders

Creative Approaches to Improving Participation: Giving Learners a Say
Helen Manchester

Turning Pupils onto Learning: Creative Classrooms in Action
Rob Elkington

Creative Learning for Inclusion: Creative Approaches to Meet Special Needs in the Classroom
Edward Sellman

Developing a Creative Curriculum: Innovative Teachers at Work
Nick Owen

Creative Learning for Inclusion

Creative approaches to meet special needs in the classroom

Edited by Edward Sellman

Routledge
Taylor & Francis Group

LONDON AND NEW YORK

First published 2012
by Routledge
2 Park Square, Milton Park, Abingdon, Oxon OX14 4RN

Simultaneously published in the USA and Canada
by Routledge
711 Third Avenue, New York, NY 10017

Routledge is an imprint of the Taylor & Francis Group, an informa business

British Library Cataloguing in Publication Data
A catalogue record for this book is available from the British Library

Library of Congress Cataloging in Publication Data
Creative learning to meet special needs : creative approaches in the classroom / [edited by] Edward Sellman.
p. cm. — (Creative teaching/creative schools)
Includes bibliographical references and index.
1. Children with disabilities—Education. 2. Creative ability—Study and teaching. 3. Creative teaching. 4. Inclusive education. I. Sellman, Edward.
LC4015.C655 2011
371.9'046—dc22
2011013493

ISBN: 978–0–415–57080–0 (hbk)
ISBN: 978–0–415–57081–7 (pbk)
ISBN: 978–0–203–81814–5 (ebk)

Typeset in Galliard
by Keystroke, Station Road, Codsall, Wolverhampton

MIX
Paper from
responsible sources
FSC
www.fsc.org **FSC® C004839**

Printed and bound in Great Britain by the MPG Books Group

For Levi

Contents

Acknowledgements

I would like to thank Pat, Julian and Naranee for their help and guidance in preparing this volume and Pat in particular for editorial assistance. I would also like to thank all the participating schools, authors, creative partners and young people who have helped write this book. Finally, gratitude is expressed to Creativity, Culture and Education (CCE) for funding each of the chapters' authors the time away from their practice to write their chapters. These acknowledgements are also echoed by each of the chapters' authors.

About the editor

Edward Sellman is a Lecturer in Special Educational Needs at the University of Nottingham and a prize winning artist. He has previously taught students experiencing emotional and behavioural difficulties and currently researches peer support and empowerment alongside the arts and creativity.

Image acknowledgements

Front cover   Alex Hallowes
Figure 2.1   Clip art images used with the permission of Microsoft.com
Figure 3.1   Mike Bartaby/Darlington Education Village
Figures 3.6a–d   Edward Sellman
Figures 4.1, 4.2 and 4.5   Alex Hallowes
Figures 5.1–5.3   Mike Scott
Figures 6.1–6.3 and 6.6   Wendy Johnson
Figure 6.7 b/c   Betti Copperwood, Wendy Johnson & Rosehill School
Figure 7.2   Thomas Tallis School
Figure 8.5   Oak Field School/Brook Publications
Figure 8.6   Mary Kirby/Phillip Pearson
Figure 8.7   Michelle Cafferkey
Figures 8.8   Mary Kirby

All figures are otherwise copyright of the chapter's author(s).

Acronyms

ADHD	Attention Deficit Hyperactivity Disorder
ASD	Autistic Spectrum Disorder
BSL	British Sign Language
CP	Creative Partnerships
CPD	Continuing Professional Development
ICT	Information Communication Technology
NACCCE	National Advisory Committee on Creative and Cultural Education
Ofsted	Office for Standards in Education
PD	Physical Disability
PIVATS	Performance Indicators for Value Added Target Setting
PLTS	Personal, Learning and Thinking Skills
PMLD	Profound and Multiple Learning Difficulties
PSHE	Personal, Social and Health Education
RSA	Royal Society for the Encouragement of Arts
SEAL	Social, Emotional Aspects of Learning
SEBD	Social, Emotional and Behavioural Difficulties
SLD	Severe Learning Difficulties
TEACCH	Treatment and Education of Autistic and Related Communication Handicapped Children

Chapter 1

Series introduction

Pat Thomson and Julian Sefton-Green

We live in creative times. As political aspiration, as economic driver, as a manifesto for school reform and curriculum change, the desire for creativity can be found across the developed world in policy pronouncements and academic research. But creativity in schools can mean many things: turning classrooms into more exciting experiences, curriculum into more thoughtful challenges, teachers into different kinds of instructors, assessment into more authentic processes and putting young people's voice at the heart of learning. In general, these aspirations are motivated by two key concerns – to make experience at school more exciting, relevant, challenging and dynamic; and ensuring that young people are able to contribute to the creative economy which will underpin growth in the twenty-first century.

Transforming these common aspirations into informed practice is not easy. Yet there are programmes, projects and initiatives which have consistently attempted to offer change and transformation. There are significant creativity programmes in many parts of the world, including France, Norway, Canada, South Korea, Australia and the United States of America. The English programme, Creative Partnerships (http://www.creative-partnerships.com) is the largest of these and this series of books draws on its experience and expertise.

This book, *Creative Learning for Inclusion*, is one of a series of books, *Creative Teaching/ Creative Schools*. The series is written for headteachers, curriculum co-coordinators and classroom practitioners who are interested in creative learning and teaching. Each book offers principles for changing classroom and school practice and stimulus material for CPD sessions. The emphasis is on practical, accessible studies from real schools, framed by jargon-free understandings of key issues and the principles found in more academic studies. Each volume contains six detailed 'case studies' written by practising teachers and other creative practitioners each describing a project they have introduced in their schools.

What is creative learning?

When educators talk about creative learning they generally mean teaching which allows students to use their imaginations, have ideas, generate multiple possible solutions to problems, communicate in a variety of media and in general 'think outside the box'. They may also mean practices in which children and young people show that they have the capacities to assess and improve work, sustain effort on a project for a long period of time, exceed what they thought was possible and work well with others to combine ideas and approaches. Some may extend the notion to include projects and approaches which allow young people to apply their creativity through making choices about what and how they will learn, negotiating about curriculum and involvement in generating possibilities for and making decisions about school priorities and directions.

But while there may be commonalities about what creative learning looks like regarding students' behaviours, there may also be profound differences. The notion of creativity may be associated with particular subjects, such as those that go under the umbrella term of the arts, in which generating new, odd and interesting perspectives on familiar topics is valued and rewarded. Or it may be seen as integral to science where habits of transforming curiosity into hypotheses have a long history. Or it may be connected to business and the goal of schooling students to have strongly entrepreneurial dispositions and capacities. These inter-pretations – and many more – are all possible and legitimate understandings of creativity and creative learning.

Although the term 'creative learning' may be new and fashionable, it draws on older knowledge and values which have helped give it legitimacy and which frame its current meaning (see Sefton-Green *et al.* 2011 and Sefton-Green and Thomson 2010). We have expressed our understanding of Creative Learning as a series of 'manifesto' principles. They underpin all the volumes in this series. Students' creative learning depends on a quality of education where:

- all young people from every kind of background are equally recognised as being creative
- learning engages young people in serious, meaningful, relevant, imaginative and chal-lenging activities and tasks
- young people are respected for their knowledge, experience and capabilities
- young people have an individual and collective right to actively shape their education
- teachers have the power to support, adapt and evaluate learning experiences for students exercising their professional judgement
- schools invest in teacher learning
- schools build partnerships with creative individuals and organisations
- schools enable young people to participate fully in social and cultural worlds
- families and local communities can play an inspiring and purposeful role in young people's learning.

Creative learning for inclusion

This book explores the role of creative learning in meeting special needs in the classroom. Edward Sellman outlines the practical challenges teachers working in both mainstream and special schools face in their classrooms and the conceptual issues which frame successful learning for young people with special needs. This book has collected together six accounts of creative approaches to inclusion, interspersed with questions to provoke discussion and debate. The case studies are written by teachers and creative practitioners, each one exploring a different theme: the importance of location and context, early years, sustainability of practice, the assessment of learning, creative uses of technology, and student participation.

References

Sefton-Green, J. and Thomson, P. (2010) *Researching Creative Learning: Methods and Issues*, London: Routledge.
Sefton-Green, J., Thomson, P., Jones, K. and Bresler, L. (eds) (2011) *The Routledge International Handbook of Creative Learning*, London: Routledge.

Chapter 2

Creative approaches to inclusion

Edward Sellman

This book is about two areas of creativity. It concerns the role creative learning can play in meeting a range of special needs but it also looks at how children with special needs can experience being creative. Whilst good practice doubtlessly exists in many places, there has been little written on this topic and this book aims to collate some exciting examples of how creativity has been applied to innovative and inclusive practice, which should help the reader begin to identify opportunities for development within their own setting. Given this aim, this book has a practical focus and is equally appropriate for mainstream and special school teachers, school leaders, professionals from children's services as well as researchers. The book contains examples of practice in mainstream and special schools but each chapter is written with professionals working in both contexts in mind.

It is necessary at the outset to stress the diverse and contested nature of what is commonly referred to as special needs. The concept spans everything from a minor problem with reading to profound and multiple learning difficulties, sometimes with an accompanying physical disability. There is also a category of social, emotional and behavioural difficulties that may or may not be present with other conditions, as well as a gifted and talented group. As a result of this breadth it is not possible for this book to adequately capture the diversity of everybody with special needs. Instead, you will read an exploration of special needs issues in the form of six case studies, all of which have been involved in one way or another in some form of creative partnership and school change project.

As the 'special needs' population is not a homogenous group, no single strategy exists, creative or not, that will meet the needs of every learner with special needs. Even a group from within the spectrum, attracting a label such as being deaf, is unlikely to possess identical needs and characteristics (see Figure 7.1 (page 69) as an illustration). Take the debated term of dyslexia as another example; it is likely this term actually captures three distinct subgroups, those who have difficulty deciphering text, those with a phonological difficulty and those with more general organisational difficulties, and any mix of these three groups. Hence, if I were to introduce you to a student with dyslexia and ask you to support their needs, I'd expect you to be confused and quite rightly ask for more detailed information. The purpose of this book is not to dispense different strategies that work well with different groups. Instead, the six case study schools will share their accounts of steps they've taken to respond to various challenges from which others can learn. Each chapter includes reflective questions and further staff development ideas to aid this process.

Nonetheless, this book does seek to identify a number of themes that may help schools develop both more creative and inclusive practice. I present a review of literature, identifying and introducing matters to consider. These themes have much in common with those cutting across the series of books of which this text is just one volume. Issues of leadership, curriculum design and assessment, amongst others, are also relevant here and are incorporated into the issues covered by the six case study chapters. Seven themes transcending the chapters of this book and discussed within this introduction are:

- the issue of location, context and physical environment
- characteristics of creative teachers and inclusive classrooms
- a developmental view of the child with special needs and personalised learning
- creativity and the curriculum
- making learning visible
- the centrality of communication
- voice and empowerment.

The introduction will then conclude with some guidance on how to use this book.

The issue of location, context and physical environment

The place in which a child is to be educated and how that physical space is going to be organised are key issues for meeting special needs. Readers may well be familiar with the difference between the concepts of integration (physical inclusion of children with special needs in the same building) and the more ambitious notion of inclusion (all children participating together in shared activities with common objectives). The merits and limitations of full inclusion against special education have been debated for well over 30 years and they continue to be so (see Hodkinson and Vickerman 2009). Thomas and Loxley (2001) and Rogers (2007) emphasise policy tensions affecting government legislation witnessed since the 1988 Education Act, which have championed integration on one hand but thwarted inclusive experiences on the other due to a curriculum designed to fit 'all' and little room for creative teaching due to rigid teaching and testing. A recent report by Ofsted (2006b) that posed the question 'Does it matter where pupils are taught?' concluded that although resourced provision fared most favourably, the issue of location is less important than other key variables such as the professionals working with young people, their skills and the types of relationships they build with their students. It also emphasised the lack of progress made over recent decades to identify and support students with special needs adequately, hence the dire need for creative approaches.

Aside from the issue of integration/inclusion, the nature of the environment also concerns how the needs of children with special needs are met. Many students with special needs benefit from safe, structured and predictable environments. This is common in schools applying such models as TEACCH (Mesibov, Shea and Schopler 2005) to meet the needs of learners on the autistic spectrum, which visually orders the physical space and timeline of the day, privatises workspace and sequences tasks to be completed. The needs of such learners, as framed by such learning environments, challenge teachers wanting to develop creative practice, which can flirt with risk and unpredictability (Chapter 5 explores these and similar issues). Other less structured contexts can be seemingly more conducive to creativity, allowing children to learn through free play and exploration and thus control the direction and pace of learning much more themselves.

Both issues of location and physical environment are examined in innovative and creative ways by several cases in this book. Chapter 3 shares its experience of a federated approach to education, where students from both special and mainstream schools have the opportunity for some co-education. In Chapters 4 and 6, the physical environment is utilised as a creative resource and both chapters capture how children with special needs interact differently with open and multi-sensory spaces respectively, alongside less structured activities. The CPD activities contained at the end of these chapters are also pertinent to schools and other contexts wishing to explore these issues.

Characteristics of creative teachers and inclusive classrooms

Given the challenges faced by those working with special needs individuals and groups, creative approaches and solutions often have to be found in order to meet students' everyday needs and/or to translate conventional curriculum and teaching methods into formats and approaches that will 'work' with them. As a result, the special needs teacher has created or adapted a multitude of artefacts: the visual timetable to support the needs of children with autism or ADHD, a multitude of communicational aids, the sand tray to reinforce multi-sensory approaches to spelling and so on. Many of these 'creations' have often found their way into a mainstream context as what turns out to be effective for individuals with special needs is also often more generally effective (Lewis and Norwich 2005). The approaches underpinning the concept of a 'Dyslexia Friendly Classroom' (Pavey 2006) are one example of this, which incorporate structured and multi-sensory strategies into standard teaching methods that are suitable for all. Any teacher however, including those working with special needs, may be eager to enhance their understanding of creativity and their skills in applying and developing its potential.

One could say that the creative teacher is also the critical teacher and it is noteworthy how most of the case studies in this book highlight this characteristic. This does not mean creative teachers go around opposing every decision and criticising their students and colleagues. It simply means that such a teacher is a reflective practitioner and applies the skills of criticality to what and how they teach, and the broader context in which their practice takes place. Such a teacher understands that the field of special needs is often inhabited by controversies, such as how a developmental disorder is diagnosed and even differentiated from others. As a result they may well have a theoretical position about certain issues, which they can defend with evidence. They will problematise their practice and context, perhaps asking such difficult questions as 'Is a student being educated in the most suitable place/ group?', 'Is their current provision adequately meeting their needs?' If it isn't, 'How can this practice be improved in their best interests?'

One of the early problems with the work of Creative Partnerships (CP), the flagship creative learning programme introduced by the UK government to promote relationships between schools and creative partners, was that its approach to inclusion was to help children fit into the existing curriculum rather than challenging the curriculum itself (Hall and Thomson 2007). More recent Creative Partnerships work, and that described in this book, has taken a more critical stance, encouraging teachers and schools to go beyond this and reshape the curriculum where there are good grounds to do so. Regarding a student with special needs, Davies (2004) suggests that a creative teacher understands a learner's needs, possesses the ability to read these, takes balanced risks and has the ability to monitor these processes. Such a teacher may challenge the structures and pedagogical approaches affecting their practice and is willing to experiment with different approaches. Successful and creative teachers will also want to bring out the same kind of capabilities in their students too.

Some of these points are also raised by Craft (2003) who reminds us that there are several policy contradictions and school-based barriers confronting teachers' creativity. These include the 'usual suspects': a narrow curriculum with its focus on testing and the centralisation (and associated de-professionalisation) of pedagogical approaches. A potential tension occurs when a teacher wishing to be creative develops a non-conventional approach, when schools are generally better suited to rewarding and reproducing conventionality. Amongst their own students, teachers frequently enjoy the products of creativity but may still find non-conformity a threat. For some, and in notable reports by NACCCE (1999) and Ofsted (2003), it is suggested that it is possible to blend creativity and discipline, retain control whilst simultaneously letting go, all whilst still delivering the national curriculum and its key objectives. However, this stance may represent a lack of ambition for many and be difficult to achieve. Balancing creativity and the occasional need to modify existing structures whilst staying loyal to national educational priorities, especially in special needs contexts where these sometimes simply do not apply, remains a challenge for many.

In one way or another, all the cases in this book share practice that involve creative teaching. This could be by radically modifying the curriculum and traditional grouping strategies, as in Chapter 3, allowing students the freedom to explore and create their own curriculum in Chapter 4, or enriching the curriculum through the arts in Chapter 5. Or it might be introducing video and observation as an assessment strategy in Chapter 6, allowing students to create their own videos and comic strips with ICT to demonstrate their learning in Chapter 7, or focusing on key life skills including voice in Chapter 8.

A developmental view of the child with special needs and personalised learning

One key element of supporting students with special needs is the observation that there may be a discrepancy between a student's age and/or physical appearance and what they are able to do independently. This often means that an educational approach needs adjustment to enable children and young people to fully access the material or engage with the material at an appropriate level. Many schools achieve this by concentrating on a developmental model of the student and making this the focus of their practice rather than what a typical child of comparable age/appearance 'should' be able to do. Sometimes this involves asking the critical question 'What counts as a relevant curriculum for our students and their needs?', involving an adjustment in curriculum priorities, such as the common emphasis on skills for independent living found at many special schools. For many special needs educators, providing a 'relevant' curriculum demands a personalised approach or person-centred planning as illustrated in Chapters 4 and 6, where students lead their own learning by identifying objects of interest to them, which teachers then responded to. This is key to Craft (2005), who insists that a creative classroom affords children a key role in sharing decisions about pedagogy, where students' interests shape lessons and provide resources.

Despite a range of critique accompanying the literature on the application of Gardner's theory of multiple intelligences (Gardner 1993) and its common bedfellow learning styles theory, these ideas have proved popular with teachers and have equipped teachers with some useful concepts for challenging the way they think about an individual's abilities and approaches to learning content. Perhaps the success of these approaches has been in challenging a language of deficit (the special needs child as inadequately developed, a typical child minus certain capabilities) and offering an alternative language of difference (the special needs child as developed differently, with their own unique profile of strengths and weaknesses). Utilising such ideas has helped many teachers to think of their students with special needs as possessing capability and agency, which counts as a starting point for further development through education. This is consistent with views of children as already resourced with creative ability, i.e. rich in experience and intrinsically motivated to explore and control their environments and the learning potential within them (Berger 2006). And it is oppositional to the 'blank slate' view of children, assumed by a 'transmission' or 'delivery' model of education, which extrinsically rewards students who reproduce desired knowledge with grades.

Some caution is necessary when adjusting or differentiating material for children with special needs, restricting the pace of their education or even adopting a child-centred model of 'free' education, as these approaches can run the risk of either dumbing down materials unnecessarily or excluding students from access to higher-level learning. Consider how Professor Stephen Hawking, assuming he wasn't famous and his computer-aided voice machine was not switched on, would be greeted at an institution such as a school, museum or gallery. Here, it is all too easy to make a correlation between apparent special need or disability and a need for simplified content, which could be completely unjustified.

Creativity and the curriculum

There are two elements to curriculum considerations in this book. One concerns creativity in its own right and initiatives taken to help children develop their own creative approaches. The other concerns the use of the arts in particular, alongside other creative approaches, to enrich the curriculum so it is both accessible and enjoyable.

One way in which the curriculum can be brought to life is through creative partnerships, well described in all chapters and in Chapter 5 in particular. These can offer fresh perspectives and sometimes a fresh start for children too. Projects undertaken with creative practitioners can lead to extended concentration on topics, improved motivation and increased engagement with curriculum areas that have been bought to life or completely repackaged (Ofsted 2006a). According to NACCCE (1999) and Davies (2004), both policy ventures, 'Excellence and Enjoyment' in relation to the curriculum and the 'Creative Partnerships' initiative, reveal a concern that the delivery of the national curriculum in many schools' approach has been rather prescriptive and dull. Broader analysis (e.g. NACCCE 1999, Hall and Thomson 2007, Banaji and Burn 2010) suggests it is economically attractive to encapsulate creativity into the curriculum as it may well be a key labour market skill for the future. Sefton-Green (2008) describes this as a form of 'neo-behaviourism'. It is not the exceptional creativity of talented individuals that is being promoted, rather an everyday creativity, or competency, to think flexibly, innovate and adapt as required by post-manufacturing and uncertain economies.

A devil's advocate view such as that briefly posed by Craft (2003) might even question the wisdom of teaching creativity at all. Given that a lot of life is monotonous and many potential careers are dull is it not, the argument goes, counterproductive to produce a generation of entertainment-seeking inquisitives who want more from life? Their situation is compounded by 'qualification inflation', where work in call centres usually requires a degree in current economic circumstances.

Whilst sharing some of these concerns, many educators including Robinson (2001) and myself see creativity as inherently worthwhile as well as economically advantageous. This is a view of the creative person as a more fulfilled person. Certainly, the cases described in this book approach creativity as both an entitlement in itself and a way of enriching the curriculum, particularly given the challenges faced by some of their students to access material in the absence of experience and multi-sensory stimulation. This is a theme common to Chapters 4, 5 and 6. It is also relevant to Chapter 3, where an alternative curriculum was instigated to put creative processes at its heart.

Making learning visible as an assessment strategy

Children with special needs often communicate both their intentions and their learning in different ways; see Table 8.2 (page 82) for an example of the ways in which children with severe learning difficulties may express themselves. A creative teacher hence needs to be receptive to and skilled in understanding these cues, which are often very subtle. One effective approach to understanding behaviour focuses on functionality. Behaviour that is challenging to manage may actually be a means of communicating distress, a need for greater help or control or another emotional state. Common responses to behaviour perceived as challenging, such as punitive responses, are thus counterproductive. It is anti-educational to punish an anxious child for example. The key lesson here is that in the absence of language, literacy or communicative competence, children will find alternative ways to communicate important messages, requiring creative approaches to both observation and interpretation. Hence, it may be helpful to ask questions such as 'What is actually happening here?' and 'What might the child be asking for?'

Balshaw (2004) highlights how working with creative practitioners can help focus a school's attention on what children can do rather than their difficulties or disabilities. This is akin to a focus on what *is* communicated rather than what *isn't*. As well as the need to focus on what is actually taking place (as explored through observation and video work in Chapters 4 and 6 respectively) it is also important to explore ways of assessment that allow students to express themselves and their learning in their preferred modality, in BSL supported video work or storyboarding as described in Chapter 7 for example.

One of the challenges of the national curriculum for many students with special needs, particularly learning difficulties or disabilities, is that its level descriptors are too advanced for some students and there are large undefined gaps of attainment in between. Hence, Lancashire County Council (1999) developed Performance Indicators for Value Added Target Setting (PIVATS) as an attempt to articulate more developmentally appropriate levels of achievement for some special needs students with tiny steps occupying the spaces in between. Not forgetting my prior warning about the risk of dumbing down the curriculum unnecessarily, this can be seen as an attempt to support teachers to observe and articulate the types of learning that they knew were taking place but lacked an appropriate framework to refer to and guidance as to where to seek evidence of development.

Clearly it is difficult to codify creativity itself but there is a well-documented (Ofsted 2006a) need to improve monitoring in this area alongside the dissemination of good practice concerning partnership working. Evaluation frameworks need to go well beyond the oft-cited improvements in ambiguous and fits-all type concepts such as 'self-esteem' and 'confidence' to more sensitive, and broader, forms of evidence capture, be these of academic or social terms of reference. These could include visual evidence (e.g. a portfolio of photographs) showing the acquisition of new technical skills and group cooperation taking place (see Ellis and Barrs 2008 for an example of one such effort to provide a framework to assess pupils' creative learning).

The centrality of communication

As just described, assessment and communication are integrated concerns for those working with children with special needs. The centrality of communication is emphasised by case study chapters in this book (particularly Chapters 4, 7 and 8). Consider this example as a means of illustrating its centrality. If I were to read the following extract to you, unless you were a speaker of Italian, you'd have little clue about what these lesson instructions contained.

> Buon mattino studenti. Oggi faciamo una gita allo zoo. Partiremo col Pullman alle nove. Ricordate di portare la vostra giacca, macchina fotografica ed il pranzo al sacco. Potete spendere solo due sterline e dovete stare in gruppo di sei persone . . .

However, if I read you the same text accompanied by the following set of clip-art pictures (props work even better), I'm confident you would get the message that we were going by coach to a zoo today and what you would need to bring (see Figure 2.1).

This example highlights two fundamental elements of creative teaching to meet special needs: structure and visualisation. A range of technical and less technical, formal and informal devices can be used to enhance communication with students with special needs. These can be adapted from existing resources or, where not available, developed from scratch. The practice of giving students the opportunity to express themselves in their preferred means of communication will be shared in Chapter 7 and creative approaches to translating or illustrating information for students with special needs feature in several other case study chapters. Communication also raises issues of voice and empowerment, which is the last theme I'd like to discuss in this introduction.

Issues of voice and empowerment[1]

The United Nations Convention on the Human Rights of the Child and multiple government guidance advocates or requires students to be consulted about decisions made about them, including students with special needs who are often the subject of various planning documents such as statements, individual education plans and annual reviews. To do this, though, frequently involves creative approaches to gauge young people's views or even roles for advocates where this is extremely challenging. Some schools are wary of conceding too much power to students or underestimate the degree of cultural change that such concessions actually require. Others suspect that voice work is a waste of time and resources, but in both published research and in my own experience this is far from the case. Instead, students tend to reward opportunities for feedback with honest, fair and constructive responses. For me the value was underlined when a 'students as researchers' team from a SEBD school reviewed their school's behaviour management policy in parallel with members of staff (Sellman 2009). Whilst the staff review concluded that the policy only

1	Buon mattino studenti.	
2	Oggi faciamo una gita allo zoo.	
3	Partiremo col Pullman. . .	
4	. . . alle nove.	
5	Ricordate di portare. . .	
6	. . . la vostra giacca,	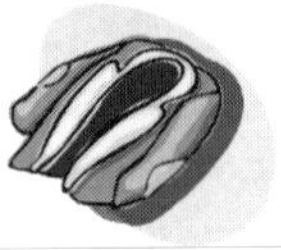
7	macchina fotografica. . . .	
8	ed il pranzo al sacco.	
9	Potete spendere solo due sterline	
10	e dovete stare in gruppo di sei persone.	

Figure 2.1 Instructions in Italian with pictures

warranted grammatical changes, the students unearthed issues of power, communication, consistency and relationships. In light of the fact that this setting also used physical interventions, the ethical dimension to seeking such feedback cannot be underestimated.

People with special needs and disabilities are more likely, according to Rix (2003), to be the objects of the creative products of culture rather than creators of cultural products themselves. In fact, cultural media is often complicit in presenting models of people with special needs as in deficit or dangerous. One then has to guard against the danger that creative activities in schools for students with special needs are purely therapeutic, which despite the best of intentions will only reproduce notions of disability. Chapter 5 gives a good account of one school's attempt to move beyond the 'show and go' nature of arts projects in schools. Chapters 7 and 8 report publications co-produced by students with special needs, setting the record straight about what life is really like for these groups.

There is also evidence (e.g. Anglia Ruskin/UCLan 2007) that arts projects can do much to alleviate the distress and marginalisation experienced by some with special needs and disability as well as help them make and build social relationships. Creative learning projects miss an opportunity if their foci are only short term. Creative engagement can be transformative, for both individuals with special needs involved in the project and other students taking part alongside them or as audience members, whose attitudes may also be transformed by the process. In fact, Anglia Ruskin/UCLan (2007) showed arts projects had more impact on pupil empowerment than they did at delivering content. The case study from Chapter 8 is pertinent here, as it shows how voice has permeated a range of practices at a special school, culminating in this voice reaching well beyond the school community to local schools and even international conferences.

To summarise this theme and the introduction as a whole, the literature and each chapter contained within this book suggest the need for a paradigm shift from instrumental approaches focused on product or performance delivery to more sustainable, holistic and partnership-based working practices focused on building inclusive communities, in which creativity plays a central role as catalyst for change.

How to use this book

Each subsequent chapter is based on a case study, which was commissioned by the author and series editors after a search of a database of schools working with CP and companion documents looking for examples of excellent practice in relation to the book's themes.

These texts have been written by school staff and creative practitioners in partnership with the editor, with multiple drafts being sent back and forth. Guidance was given on foci, reflexivity and format, to encourage a similar structure and tone to each of the case studies, whilst also staying true to the personalised nature of the accounts being shared. Some editing has taken place in agreement with each author to help the reader navigate the chapters by giving each a style.

Hence, within each chapter there are common features:

- an articulation of the challenge
- a timeline of the project undertaken
- the account itself
- key learning points.

At the end of the chapter there are relevant resources, which the reader may find helpful for locating extra information or reading further about issues introduced within the chapter. There is also at least one suggested CPD exercise, which can be used by schools and other settings to examine and/or further investigate the themes discussed in each chapter in relation to the reader's own context. Each chapter can of course be used as a case study for CPD in its own right.

Each chapter begins and concludes with a commentary from the editor to help relate issues discussed to others and focus the reader's attention on particular points. Boxed comments are also inserted within the text to enhance this commentary, raising questions for further consideration or suggesting areas for CPD.

I hope you choose to read the entire book as it has been written to give an overview of creative and innovative practice. However, Figure 2.2 is provided as detailed guidance on the book's contents, showing the characteristics of the settings in which each case study is located and the themes explicitly or implicitly covered by each chapter. This may be helpful in identifying a focus of interest or pinpointing a case study for CPD purposes.

Note

1   For more on this topic, see Helen Manchester's book in this series, titled *Creative Approaches to Improving Participation: Giving Learners a Say* (Routledge, 2011).

References

Anglia Ruskin/UCLan (2007) *Mental Health, Social Inclusion and the Arts*, London: Social Inclusion.

Balshaw, M. (2004) Risking creativity: building the creative context, *Support for Learning*, 19 (2), 71–76.

Banaji, S. and Burn, A. with Buckingham, D. (2010) *The Rhetorics of Creativity: A Literature Review*. 2nd edn. Newcastle: Creativity, Culture and Education.

Berger, R. (2006) Using contact with nature, creativity and rituals as a therapeutic medium with children with learning difficulties: a case study, *Emotional and Behavioural Difficulties*, 11 (2), 135–146.

Craft, A. (2003) The limits to creativity in education: dilemmas for the educator, *British Journal of Educational Studies*, 51 (2), 113–127.

Craft, A. (2005) *Creativity in Schools: Tensions and Dilemmas*, Abingdon: RoutledgeFalmer.

Davies, D. (2004) Creative teachers for creative learners – a literature review. *Teacher Training Resource Bank*, available online at: http://www.ttrb.ac.uk/attachments/c3096c7b-da04-41ef-a7ac-50535 306e8fb.pdf (accessed 30/09/2010; no longer available).

Ellis, S. and Barrs, M. (2008) The assessment of creative learning, in Sefton-Green, J. (2008) (ed.) *Creative Learning*, London: Arts Council/Creative Partnerships, pp. 74–89.

Gardner, H. (1993) *Frames of Mind: The Theory of Multiple Intelligences*, New York: Basic Books.

Hall, C. and Thomson, P. (2007) Creative partnerships? Cultural policy and inclusive arts practice in one primary school, *British Educational Research Journal*, 33 (3), 315–329.

Hodkinson, A. and Vickerman, P. (2009) *Key Issues in Special Educational Needs and Inclusion*, London: Sage.

Lancashire County Council (1999) *PIVATS*, information available online at: http://www.lancashire. gov.uk/education/pivats/ (accessed 30/09/2010).

Lewis, A. and Norwich, B. (2005) *Special Teaching for Special Children? Pedagogies for Inclusion*, Buckingham: Open University Press.

Mesibov, G., Shea, V. and Schopler, E. (2005) *The TEACCH Approach to Autism Spectrum Disorders*, New York: Springer.

Figure 2.2 Overview of case study chapters

	Chapter 3: Darlington Education Village	Chapter 4: McMillan	Chapter 5: Brays	Chapter 6: Rosehill	Chapter 7: Thomas Tallis	Chapter 8: Oak Field
School type	Federation (mainstream primary, secondary and special provision)	Mainstream nursery	Special	Special	Mainstream secondary	Special
Age range focus	11–14	3–5	3–11	5–19	11–16	3–19
Special needs focus	Mixed	Mixed	Moderate and severe learning difficulties & physical disability	Autistic spectrum disorders	Deaf students/ students with hearing impairments	Severe learning difficulties & physical disability
Location/ Context/ Environment theme	♦	◊		◊		
Creative teaching/ classrooms theme	◊	♦	◊		♦	
Developmental view/ personalised learning theme	♦	♦				
Curriculum enrichment theme	◊		♦	◊		◊
Learning visibility theme		◊		♦	◊	
Communication theme					♦	♦
Voice/ empowerment theme					♦	♦
Other themes central to chapter			Sustain-ability	Sustain-ability	ICT	Sex/relation ships educa-tion, social needs

Key: ♦ main theme ◊ subsidiary theme

National Advisory Committee on Creative and Cultural Education (NACCCE) (1999) *All Our Futures: Creativity, Culture and Education*, London: Department for Education and Employment/Department for Culture Media and Sport.

Ofsted (2003) *Expecting the Unexpected: Developing Creativity in Primary and Secondary Schools* (Ref HMI 1612) London: Ofsted.

Ofsted (2006a) *Creative Partnerships: Initiative and Impact* (Ref HMI 2517), London: Ofsted.

Ofsted (2006b) *Inclusion: Does it Matter Where Pupils are Taught? – Provision and Outcomes in Different Settings for Pupils with Learning Difficulties and Disabilities* (Ref HMI 2535), London: Ofsted.

Pavey, B. (2006) *The Dyslexia-Friendly Primary School: A Practical Guide for Teachers*, London: Sage.

Rix, P. (2003) 'Anything is possible': the arts and social inclusion, *Policy Futures in Education*, 1 (4), 716–730.

Robinson, K (2001) *Out of Our Minds: Learning to be Creative*, Chichester: Capstone.

Rogers, C. (2007) Experiencing an 'inclusive' education: parents and their children with 'special educational needs', *British Journal of Sociology of Education*, 28 (1), 55–68.

Sefton-Green, J. (2008) (ed.) *Creative Learning*, London: Arts Council/Creative Partnerships.

Sellman, E. (2009) Lessons learned: student voice at a school for pupils experiencing social, emotional and behavioural difficulties, *Emotional and Behavioural Difficulties*, 14(1), 33–48.

Thomas, G. and Loxley, A. (2001) *Deconstructing Special Education and Constructing Inclusion*, Buckingham: Open University Press.

Creative school organisation and curriculum

Rachel Ireland, Darlington Education Village

Editor's introduction

This chapter describes an innovative approach to developing an inclusive school community and curriculum at Darlington Education Village, a federation of one special and two former primary and secondary mainstream schools on the same site. It focuses on an account of a thematic approach to the curriculum allowing students aged 11–14 opportunities to work alongside others with different needs on extended projects.

HOW TO USE THIS CHAPTER

The insights shared in this chapter will challenge professionals working with children and young people in any educational context to think creatively about:

- how special and mainstream provision is organised
- how structures can be changed to bring students into contact with a greater variety of learners
- the degree of cultural consistency underpinning different forms of provision, particularly after an amalgamation
- how transition from one form of provision to another could be made smoother and more coherent
- how a more inclusive community can be developed.

The school context

The Education Village is a pioneering project in its own right, being the first fully federated and integrated education village, serving 1,400 children and young people aged 2–19 in the north-east of England. The village was formed from Springfield Primary School, Haughton Community School and Arts College, and Beaumont Hill Technology and Vocational College, all now located on one site. We now share many facilities and resources, which encourage interaction between children of different ages, and between mainstream pupils and those with special needs.

The Village opened in 2006 with a single leadership team and governing body. It is led by an executive director, who also acts as the headteacher for the three schools. There is a distributed model of senior and middle leadership. Six directors form a leadership team with roles for inclusion, teaching and learning, project development, engagement and pupil well-being, business strategy and community. At the next level, there are progress leaders across the three schools, who report to these directors.

Provision for special needs and inclusion is a key feature. Elements of the design help access and mobility, as well as encouraging pupils to mix. For example, the school is centred around a village green, accessible by all pupils (see Figure 3.1).

We have also installed walkways providing direct access to the first floor for wheelchair users and our corridors and shared social spaces are wide and naturally lit. We are also fortunate to enjoy considerable ICT resources.

The special school provision educates 216 pupils aged 2–19 years, from across the special needs spectrum, including:

- a department for more than 40 pupils on the autistic spectrum
- a post-16 section for students with learning difficulties, delivering the Lifeskills for Independence Curriculum
- provision for students experiencing social, emotional and/or behavioural difficulties (SEBD) for students aged 6 to 16 years.

Combining resources allows staff and pupils easier and more immediate access to a greater range of facilities than normally available at one school; these include:

- a Learning Resource Centre and library and independent learning areas
- a 25-metre swimming pool and hydrotherapy pool
- a Village Green (see Figure 3.1) for external performances and events

Figure 3.1 Village Green, the centre-point of the three schools

- well-equipped outdoor classrooms
- interactive and music therapy rooms with support bases for visiting therapists.

EDITOR'S COMMENT

It's interesting to return to the question posed in Chapter 2, 'does it matter where pupils are taught?', especially in light of some of the challenges already introduced in this chapter. Given that different forms of provision will be underpinned by different cultures, values and priorities, what might be the obstacles to building an inclusive community, especially where one school feels duty bound to raise standards and another feels it is not able to do this until other needs are met first. Inclusive community will depend heavily on the types of relationships forged between staff and pupils across the site. Can you think of any tensions here and how these might be anticipated and resolved?

The challenge

Given the Education Village's federated status, inevitably there will be numerous challenges, particularly concerning issues of leadership, consistency and overseeing a smooth transition through a period of rapid change. Some momentum was lost in this regard when the school was put under pressure to focus its attention on raising standards for external inspection, particularly in its secondary provision, a challenge only too familiar to most schools. The relocation process also placed strain on the leadership structure as there was over-representation of school leaders from one of the original schools on the new school leadership team, despite local authority guidance on ensuring rigorous and transparent appointment procedures. This caused some initial tension, which the leadership team has attempted to overcome with success.

Integrating three former schools into one community also raises issues about cultural consistency, as each culture of the former schools had different values, priorities and approaches to inclusion. The Education Village has a radical vision for inclusion, which has resulted in some tensions with parents. Some parents consulted by the school, particularly those whose children had previously attended the primary school, raised anxieties and concerns about their children interacting with older students.

Not putting any of these important issues aside, this chapter focuses on trying to develop a more inclusive curriculum. Given the relocation of one special and two mainstream schools in physical proximity, one of our very first challenges was to consider how to encourage staff and students to function as one inclusive 'village', now we shared one site. In particular, we sought to address the following issues:

- how students with different roles perceived one another
- how we could provide students with opportunities to learn about each other's needs
- how we could encourage students to respect each other.

We took the opportunity to re-design the 11–14 curriculum in order to enable students to learn together and help build an inclusive ethos. It was also necessary to ensure that staff were given opportunities to work collectively in order to develop an understanding of student needs across the provision and for this reason team-teaching was also incorporated into the curriculum design. This chapter shares our experience of innovation and the lessons we are continuing to learn along the way.

Our timeline

2002   Plans for a federated school announced
2003   Work with Creative Partnerships begins
2005   Evaluation of curriculum and leadership structures
       Student/parent consultation exercise
2006   Education Village opens
       Opening Minds curriculum introduced
2008   PLTS/SEAL integrated into the curriculum

Designing an inclusive curriculum

The Education Village's leadership and management structures are designed to put the child at the centre of provision. This has involved developing holistic approaches to multi-service delivery and to meeting outcomes concerning child well-being. Our philosophy of inclusive education is inextricably linked to the concept of 'personalisation' and the belief that all students should have optimum access to the curriculum based on their individual need and, where possible, addressed through their preferred learning styles. This is achieved through a diverse and meaningful curriculum in place, where pace and learning are matched to pupils' readiness and abilities.

For us, personalisation can be addressed in a variety of ways, such as through:

- planned adult support to assist pupils in particular lessons where appropriate
- small group extra core subject lessons delivered by trained staff
- individualised timetables that offer a flexible curriculum and access to a range of accredited courses and programmes post-14
- access to a range of skills due to the federation of three former schools and the considerable and various expertise of their staff
- state-of-the-art facilities including resourcing in new technologies
- a rigorous focus upon student achievement
- students being offered the whole experience of being a member of the Education Village and beyond in order to develop caring and concerned citizens both in the present and future.

We wanted to incorporate some of the benefits of approaches already having a positive impact post-14 into our 11–14 provision. To begin the process of re-designing an inclusive curriculum for this age group, a period of evaluation took place to gain a realistic understanding of current practices and provision across the site. Elements of good practice were identified, as were aspects that needed improving or completely re-thinking. This initial development process was led by our Deputy Head Teacher, who was experienced in curriculum design and innovation, alongside a number of key staff who would be instrumental in the delivery of the new curriculum. It was essential at this stage that staff from across the whole 'Village' were involved.

A key area that was explored at the beginning of the project was the transition between the primary and secondary phase at age 11. Prior to the federation of the three schools, the special needs provision was distributed over several sites. The mainstream primary provision was also a feeder school for the mainstream secondary school. This historical legacy reinforced a division between the primary and secondary curriculum and undermined efforts to support students with special needs. The Education Village therefore found itself in an excellent position to think creatively about new organisational structures and curriculum design, to facilitate a more positive and progressive transition for all our students.

As one component of the initial evaluation, all teaching stages within the Education Village were consulted and invited to share their views. Members of staff were also given the opportunity to think 'out of the box' and were encouraged to consider the exercise as a blank canvas upon which to redesign school life. Some key themes came out of this consultation:

- Having longer blocks of learning time
- Teaching curriculum content through engaging themes
- Developing cross-curricular projects and schemes of work
- Reducing the amount of movement for students
- Encouraging better student–teacher relationships through key teacher roles
- Encouraging greater respect between students with different needs
- Ensuring that students learned how to take responsibility for their own learning.

Parents and students from the primary phase (5–11) were also consulted about the curriculum development ideas. They were asked to share their thoughts, hopes and concerns regarding the move to secondary education (11–16). Many of the parental concerns related to fears associated with their child sharing social spaces with older children, the relationships they would form and how they would fit in. Many of the students indicated they were looking forward to making the transition but they also had concerns relating to relationships with older students and getting lost.

As a result of the evaluation and consultation exercises, a number of key curriculum aims were identified, which also had implications for social interaction. These were:

- To enable our learners to transfer and apply the skills that they have developed from one curriculum area to another.
- To provide our learners with opportunities to become more independent and take responsibility for their own learning.
- To enable our learners to be able to solve a range of problems independently and creatively.
- To provide learners with appropriate opportunities to co-construct aspects of their learning.
- To give students opportunities to work with other students with a variety of needs.

To address these key aims and the feedback from the consultation exercise, a number of innovative ideas were developed and implemented. For example, the humanities subjects, ICT and drama were to be taught in the following ways:

- as larger blocks of cross-curricular learning
- in mixed groups
- organised around themes of learning
- focused upon specific competences and skills.

This new approach was inspired by the 'Opening Minds' model developed by RSA (see resource list) and introduced to us by our relationship with Creative Partnerships (CP). Hence, our 11–12-year-old students began to receive 10 hours of study per week, dedicated to lessons from the Opening Minds programme (see Figure 3.2).

The teacher who taught these lessons to each class would be the same class tutor. This meant that students had a significant amount of time and daily contact with one key member of staff. We hoped this would encourage positive relationships to develop and help with the transition from primary to secondary phases, which is usually characterised by moving from one classroom with one teacher to multiple changes of classrooms and teachers. Students with additional difficulties normally catered for within mainstream education (e.g. students with dyslexia or ADHD for example) find this transition particularly challenging and we hoped this change would be supportive of their needs.

A school within a school

This curriculum model was initially implemented as a model for our classes for 11–12-year-olds, although as the students moved into subsequent year groups, so did the model. For us, one element of its success was the decision to pair the 'Opening Minds' lessons for each class with one teacher, who also became their form tutors. Each class was organised to ensure there was a diversity of learners in each group. Staffing was organised to facilitate a strong team approach to the curriculum, encouraging teachers with a range of relevant expertise to work together to form a 'school within a school'. Figure 3.3 shows how the staff team was structured and how expertise was distributed across the team. At the centre of the team was a Progress Leader who was responsible for the whole year group, both pastorally and academically, and was accountable to senior leadership.

We felt this curriculum approach would be more supportive for students with special needs as the thematic approach allowed students to focus on their strengths and support others. The topics covered also allowed students to make greater use of their own experience as an educational resource and interact with material that was presented in a more joined up and multisensory manner. Their needs were also aided by a good representation of special needs expertise within the teaching team.

The variety of staff expertise within this team was initially intended to ensure appropriate representation of the subject areas that were to be taught, even though these were no longer taught discreetly. However, ongoing evaluation has identified many additional benefits. Members of staff reported that they felt valued as each had an area of leadership. Working

Figure 3.2 The frequency of different lessons for our 11–12-year-old students

Opening Minds	English	Maths	Science	PE	Art & Design	Music	Design & Technology	Languages
10	3	3	2	2	1	1	2	1

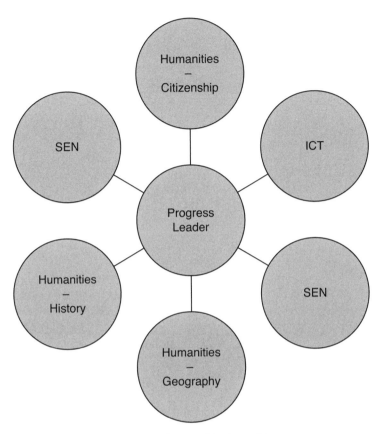

Figure 3.3 The structure of the Opening Minds teaching team

collaboratively on curriculum, assessment and moderation also strengthened the team and encouraged an ongoing process of reflection, evaluation and improvement – so it was inclusive for them as well as the pupils. This has resulted in positive changes being made to schemes of work on a regular basis. Professional development was also evident and as a direct result of stepping out of traditional subject area thinking. Staff reported that experience in teaching cross-curricular themes had also changed their teaching practice in other areas of the school and the subjects they taught. Collaboration also seemed to encourage greater problem solving of issues arising in the classroom.

Teaching PLTS through an Opening Minds curriculum for all learners

Development and integration of PLTS (personal, learning and thinking skills) has also been a key driver in the further reconstruction of the curriculum model. The school had already begun to use the language of competences when redesigning the curriculum when a second round of planning gave staff the further opportunity to integrate the RSA Opening Mind's elements with both PLTS and other competencies from the SEAL (Social and Emotional Aspects of Learning) curriculum into an elaborated model. A group of staff explored the learning behaviours that would be evident if students were demonstrating the following PLTS:

- Reflective Learners
- Effective Participators
- Self Managers
- Team Workers
- Creative Thinkers
- Independent Enquirers.

To make sure this happened, each of the PLTS was broken down into a set of behaviours and a set of further descriptors. These skills were then represented as a PLTS wheel to demonstrate that progress and application of these skills is not linear, but continual, as shown in Figure 3.4.

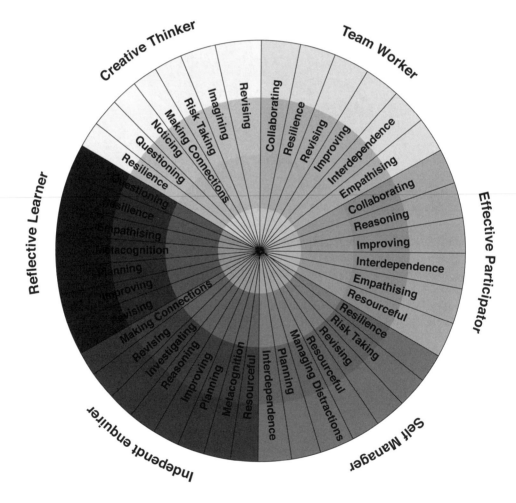

Figure 3.4 The PLTS wheel

There is a commitment and belief from staff that these reflect an invaluable set of skills that all learners should develop to enable them to be successful throughout school and in their lives outside of school. We also feel that the PLTS wheel offers a number of advantages to learners with special needs because it:

- encourages the development of a broad range of life skills such as independence and co-operation
- allows students to focus on areas of strength
- focuses on personalisation
- recognises the learner as resourceful
- is based on topics rather than abstract concepts taught out of context
- involves engaging themes which relate to real-life experience
- downplays the demands placed on a narrow range of 'traditional' academic skills
- allows all students easy opportunity to make a contribution
- develops awareness and reflexivity of the learning process.

Ensuring that staff were familiar with the Education Village PLTS model and knew how to create appropriate opportunities for learning was essential. This was done by making one of the six PLTS the focus of each half term, delivered through the context of a theme every 6–7 weeks, which was then enriched using the cross-curricular dimensions previously developed in conjunction with the 'Opening Minds' curriculum initiative (see Figure 3.5).

In order to ensure that students were experiencing consistency across the curriculum, it was important that all subject leaders collaboratively planned the PLTS and cross-curricular themes into their schemes of work. This has positively impacted upon students' ability to transfer skills and make connections from one subject area to another. Additionally members of staff have a greater understanding of each other's subject areas.

Figure 3.5 Curriculum year overview

	Personal, Learning and Thinking skills	Cross curricular dimension	Opening Minds Scheme of work
Autumn 1st half term	Reflective Learner	Healthy Lifestyles	Your Health is Your Wealth
Autumn 2nd half term	Independent Enquirer	Global dimensions & sustainability	Wasters
Spring 1st half term	Effective participators	Technology & Media	It came from the deep
Spring 2nd half term	Team workers	Enterprise	Down on the farm
Summer 1st half term	Self manager	Identity & cultural dimensions	Windows on the World
Summer 2nd half term	Creative thinkers	Creativity and critical thinking	Let's create

Delivering an inclusive curriculum

A major benefit in developing a staff team to teach the Opening Minds curriculum and PLTS has been the continual opportunities for inclusion. The team was developed with staff representatives from across the Education Village, allowing for trained and experienced SEN staff to both teach the curriculum and act as consultants to other staff. This allowed the students across the federation to be grouped according to capability and to learn alongside peers, rather than on the basis of which school they belonged to or whether they had special educational needs or not.

This is well illustrated by one group, consisting of students from two sites, coming together as one class. The students within this class had a variety of special needs including specific and moderate learning difficulties, autistic spectrum disorders and social, emotional behavioural difficulties. At the beginning of the term, the students joined one another for their Opening Minds lessons and were taught by a team of two teachers and one teaching assistant. The curriculum encouraged the students to learn not only with each other, but from each other.

The thematic approach helped students engage both with the content and their class-mates, aided by the fact that everyone had some prior and developing knowledge and understanding to share. The competence-based model ensured students developed a good understanding of working effectively alongside a variety of personalities and people with needs that were different from their own.

Key learning points

The teachers working on the Opening Minds Curriculum and PLTS have reported a number of benefits that this inclusive teaching has had, not just for students, but also for them as professionals. Staff reported an increased familiarity in working with a range of students and their different needs and a better understanding of differentiation. They also felt that the approach encouraged students of all abilities to set themselves more ambitious targets for their own learning. Some of the observed benefits for students have been:

- Learning is better matched to the needs and interests of the students.
- Students create opportunities for their own learning.
- All learners experience some success.
- Students challenge each other.
- Students bring a diversity of experiences into the curriculum.

- Students are more able to express themselves in front of peers.
- Students understand each other's strengths and weaknesses to a greater extent and are more appropriate with one another accordingly.
- Students have greater ability to communicate with other people.

These benefits are encouraging, however, they are only small steps towards greater inclusion. To give students greater opportunity to meet and learn with and from one another, a range of curriculum enrichment and community-based activities also take place, including:

- shared social spaces
- themed whole-school 'super learning' days
- mixed assemblies
- activity weeks involving the whole-school community
- learning outside the classroom
- community events.

There are areas in which the Education Village still needs to make improvements. We are working towards improving attendance, engagement with parents, and provision for 'vulnerable' students as well as reducing exclusions, and the number of young people not entering employment, education or training.

EDITOR'S COMMENT

Having read this inspiring account of innovative approaches to inclusive school organisation and curriculum, consider what strategies could be employed at your setting to encourage both:

i)   greater transference of experience and expertise between different forms of provision, and
ii) opportunities to address the secondary difficulties faced by children and young people with special needs (for example, how they are positioned in a group and attitudes to their difficulties encountered in real-life settings).

What next?

After federation and a period of rapid change, it is important to stock take and consolidate good practice whilst challenging ourselves to improve in other areas. We need to review which practices are working well and where there is room for further growth. No doubt consultation of pupil and parent views alongside those of our teachers will play a key role, as will our partnership working.

Already, the leadership team recognises that a focus on the processes that support cultural integration would be helpful for the Education Village both within our provision and our community. This process could be aided by:

- gaining a deeper understanding of leadership and governance issues affecting cultural integration
- greater communication and collaboration between colleagues to identify and establish common priorities and shared strategies
- building stronger links with our community
- aiming for fuller integration of local authority services within the village in order that our students have effective and seamless access to support when needed.

Resources

Books

Ayers, H., Clarke, D. and Murray, A. (1995) *Perspectives on Behaviour: A Practical Guide to Effective Interventions for Teachers*, London: David Fulton. This book offers practitioners a good overview about different theoretical perspectives on behaviour and features in the CPD exercise.

Moon, J. (2007) *Critical Thinking: An Exploration of Theory and Practice*, London: Routledge. This book discusses the concept of criticality. It offers frameworks for understanding different levels of criticality and shares examples of writing that illustrate these levels.

Savage, J. (2010) *Cross-Curricular Teaching and Learning in the Secondary School*, London: Routledge/David Fulton. This book is part of a series on cross-curricular teaching and learning and other volumes may be of interest too.

Wyse, D. and Dowson, P. (2009) *The Really Useful Creativity Book*, London: Routledge. This book suggests reorganising the curriculum to promote thinking skills and shares some practical tips about doing this.

Websites

Our website is available at: http://www.educationvillage.org.uk

Below are some links to external sites that you may find useful to discover more information about the RSA, Opening Minds and innovative curriculum:

- http://www.thersa.org
- http://www.futurelab.org.uk
- http://www.enquiringminds.org.uk

CPD ACTIVITY

Think about the different theoretical perspectives you are aware of for informing understanding of students' behavior, teaching and learning. Ayers, Clarke and Murray's book (see resource list) give an excellent overview of a range of perspectives, including: behavioural, cognitive-behavioural, social-learning, psychodynamic, humanistic and ecosystemic approaches. In groups, select one of these perspectives each and think about how a school or classroom would be designed along their principles. Think about the forms of interaction, opportunities for freedom and creativity, as well as the opportunities for inclusion in particular. Then, using a range of art materials create floor plans of what these environments might look like. Then feedback to colleagues to inform a discussion about how the environment affords different forms of interaction. From this discussion, identify steps that could be taken to promote inclusion in your context.

Here are some images from students at the University of Nottingham who have engaged with this exercise.

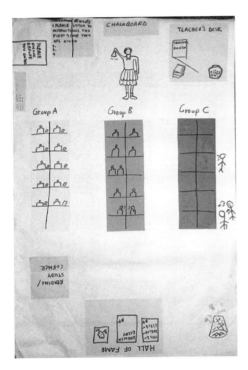

Figure 3.6a Behaviourist model of a classroom

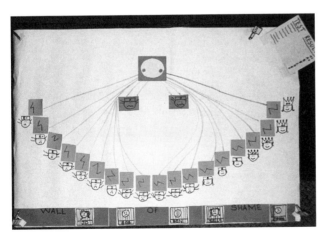

Figure 3.6b Foucauldian model of a classroom

Figure 3.6c Ecological model
of a classroom

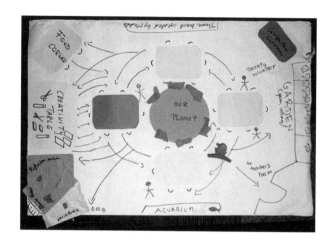

Figure 3.6d Humanistic model
of a classroom

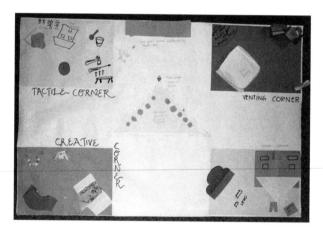

Fostering creativity in the early years

Alex Hallowes (Creative Practitioner) and Andrew Shimmin (Headteacher), McMillan Children's Centre and Nursery School, Hull

Editor's introduction

Three main factors are identified in this chapter, each essential for the success of the work described. These are:

- Time
- Partnership
- Desire.

Professionals working with children are always challenged by time – and being critically reflective does take time. A creative partnership can act as a mirror to encourage critical reflection but many projects involving artists in schools also suffer from a lack of time. This chapter describes a deep and reciprocal relationship established between a nursery school and a creative practitioner and the change process that occurred over time. The long-standing nature of the partnership afforded a relationship to develop that incorporated respect and trust, where each partner was able to challenge and question each other in a constructive manner. Change is only possible when staff desire and embrace such a partnership and the transformation it can encourage.

HOW TO USE THIS CHAPTER

This chapter describes the change process resulting from a longstanding relationship with a creative practitioner at a nursery school that wanted to offer a more child-centred and inclusive early years experience. Unlike other chapters that focus on specific issues, this chapter focuses on generally inclusive practice, and thus will be useful to both mainstream and special education contexts, particularly those who work with very young children or children with additional needs operating at an early stage of intellectual development. It reinforces the argument (see introduction) that effective special teaching is also effective general teaching and therefore inclusion is about adopting a pedagogy that allows all learners to study alongside each other. The lessons shared will be useful for any setting considering work with creative practitioners as a catalyst for significant school change.

The school context

McMillan Nursery School became a Children's Centre in 2006 and offers daycare and early years education for 150–200 children. The Nursery School is situated in an area of Hull served by a Sure Start Local Programme, helping children and families make a good start to their education even though the community faces several challenges.

Given their age, relatively few of our children have formally identified special needs but many experience difficulties, particularly in areas of communication, language and literacy development. Thus, the Nursery School also offers 'Nurture Groups', where children who have need of extra help can benefit from one-to-one support or small-group sessions and access to specific strategies or resources, whilst spending the morning with staff who have special needs training and experience. Those who stay all day join the nursery class in the afternoon. This nurture group serves a dual purpose: providing both i) focused support to children with additional difficulties whilst building their confidence in small groups and ii) opportunities to socialise in larger groups, further building their social skills.

The Nursery, now a 'School of Creativity' has a longstanding relationship with Creative Partnerships (CP). Several factors prompted our initial involvement with CP and have continued as ongoing elements in the development of our partnership work. These are a desire to be:

- proactive in developing high-quality experiences for our children and their families
- creative in challenging and developing our practice
- collaborative in working with partners.

Here follows an account of our story of change, starting with our early work with CP.

The challenge

After working with Creative Partnerships (CP) for some time, we began to question more deeply the nature of the relationship and the projects we had developed. We had attempted to address the concept of 'sustainability' suggested by CP as essential to effective change but shared a feeling that our engagement with this had hitherto been at a shallow level. We had aimed to move beyond the tokenism of one-off arts based projects and events to create 'pieces' that had some ongoing life and value in the school, but began to feel that the real sustainability was around the partnerships we had been developing with creative practitioners, and the considerable potential this had for developing and embedding new and different ways of approaching our daily practices with young children. We decided to focus on the process, rather than the product, as the core of our 'change project'.

This chapter will describe how such a process developed over time and the learning along the way. It will focus on a project called 'Eyes Wide Open', which was inspired by our encounter with the work of the Reggio Emilia Preschools and attempts to develop some of the creative, child-centred and inclusive principles of the approach in our setting with the support of CP.

Hence, our key challenges can be summarised as:

- How do we implement meaningful and sustainable change?
- How do we utilise CP as part of this change process?

Figure 4.1 A creative journey

- How do we begin to embed more creative, child-centred and inclusive approaches in our early years practices?

Our timeline

2002 Became a Creative Partnerships (CP) school, observation days for artists and small projects started.

2004 Staff visit to Reggio and began planning for Eyes Wide Open Project.

2005 Staff and artist visit to Reggio, visits to other settings and attendance at relevant conferences.
Eyes Wide Open Project starts.

2006 Dissemination of the project starts and networks established with other settings.
School becomes a Children's Centre.

2007 Ofsted identifies that outside provision needs development and CP projects adjust their focus.

2008 Staff attend 'Forest Schools' training.
Creative Partnerships 'School of Creativity' status achieved.

2009 Forest School project continues and staff give training to other early years settings.

Starting point – working with Creative Partnerships

We recognise that creativity is an important aspect of being human, it is central to learning and we have been delighted by policy attempts to position creativity as an educational priority. When central government launched Creative Partnerships, it initially focused upon what had been identified as 16 culturally and socially deprived areas of England, of which Hull was one. McMillan became a CP school in June 2002 soon after the inception of the programme.

We initially viewed the programme as an opportunity to access a funding stream for creative projects between schools and local artists but as we became more immersed in the work, and as we understood more about what CP were trying to achieve, our emphasis changed considerably. We began to look at creative learning as a 'process' rather than 'product' orientated approach with considerable potential for improving the experiences we provided for our children, especially those ill served by traditional approaches to nursery education. These include children with additional difficulties or from homes where children do not have access to much reading material and/or where English is not the first language.

Working with a creative practitioner was rewarding, yet challenging, for everybody. We were initially challenged by the suggestion that there are two sure ways to stifle creativity (See Owen's book in our resource list for further description):

The *first* way is to say 'no' to everything, to be too controlling and thus inhibit any ideas, confidence and opportunity for change.

The *second* way is to say 'yes' to everything. In this scenario, children learn that:

- there are no boundaries
- all behaviour is acceptable
- all their ideas are perfect and require no further work
- everything they do deserves lavish praise and reward.

In our experience, these children are equally disempowered – with no understanding of failure, no critical criteria for assessing their own work, no resilience for working through a problem, no questioning skills, and probably few social skills. The challenge for us was to develop a setting somewhere in between these two extremes, which required an in-depth understanding of the factors involved in inhibiting or encouraging children's creativity.

CP is underpinned by the principles of inclusivity and sustainability. In many ways, each project starts as an 'action-research' opportunity to explore these issues. In collaboration we started a project called 'Eyes Wide Open', a metaphor we chose in order to challenge ourselves to expect the unexpected and to try and see everyday practices in ways we had not seen before. The focus of this collaboration was to explore how we could develop our practice in order to include all our children in a more creative learning environment. We wanted to do this in a sustainable way rather than run another project with a predetermined output and finite lifespan, even if adjustments had been successful in the past to make it more inclusive.

We started our journey wanting to 'open our eyes' to creative opportunities which would allow our children, especially those who had difficulties with communicating ideas, to more fully engage with the curriculum we offered. To inform this process, we started by exploring alternative models of preschool education that approached children and their education from a different perspective.

Experimenting with the Reggio approach

In 1998, Angela, McMillan's previous headteacher, visited Reggio Emilia, the city in Northern Italy renowned worldwide for its early years practice. She returned inspired and determined to develop elements of the work of Reggio at McMillan. CP supported the idea that a 'Reggio' inspired project would be beneficial for the development of our creative school, and the 'Eyes Wide Open' project evolved into an artist-in-residence, focused upon looking at elements of 'Reggio' practice. Alex was appointed to this role in September 2004.

The Reggio approach views the child as already being resourceful, creative, competent and intelligent and someone who co-constructs knowledge of their world with their teacher (Moss, see resource list, provides a good description of the approach). Inspired by this conception, we invited our children to just be themselves on our project and to help us as adults learn a new way of approaching our work with them, recognising their existing competence and abilities (see Figure 4.2).

This 'invitation' to children was guided by a set of 'creative learning characteristics', developed by Anna Cutler, the Creative Partnerships' Director for the county of Kent (see resource list). These feature in the CP evaluation framework and became a matrix around which we started to think (see Figure 4.3).

Figure 4.2 Children as co-constructors of knowledge

Figure 4.3 Creative Learning Characteristics adapted from Anna Cutler

Creative learning Characteristics	Examples
Identifying problems	Asking the right kinds of questions to find out what you need to do and why; combining thought with actions; being encouraged to realise there is a problem; thinking through issues from different perspectives.
Divergent thinking	Exploring different solutions; experimenting with 'alternatives'; taking things in a different direction; being prepared to fail.
Co-learning	Working with others; collaborating; exploring a task together; sharing and listening to each others' responses and building on them; passing on ideas and knowledge.
Fascination	Being allowed to pursue one's own line of enquiry; being absorbed; curiosity; inspiration leading to action.
Risk taking	Trying things not previously attempted; joining in new activities; willing to have a go; not going for the obvious way of doing something; overcoming fear of failure; not feeling judged or judging others.
Balance of skills and challenges	Trying something out and trying again, trying the next level of difficulty; doing harder things, overcoming setbacks.
Refinement	Practising; reworking; drafting; working through ideas; developing higher standards; wanting to do better.

These characteristics informed the approach we adopted. In the initial stages of the journey, the children may not have noticed much difference as the routine of the day and the people working with them remained consistent. But, as time passed, as we relaxed more and started to explore new approaches to familiar issues, the children would have begun to notice some changes, enabling them to be more free, to take their play further and to take risks which would not have been allowed previously (see Figure 4.4).

The project had some tensions. In the early stages, Alex, our creative partner, felt frustrated with existing practices. Likewise staff had reservations on occasions about the way Alex allowed our children much more freedom and to take greater risks than we were used to. This felt very different for all involved but we learned that the boundaries that children could safely explore were a lot further away than first imagined. The fact that the school's relationship with Alex was given time to develop and staff were genuinely eager to embrace change meant that both sides learned how to support each other.

In a questionnaire delivered to staff in December 2009, many staff considered that although their practice had been good prior to the Eyes Wide Open initiative, the project enabled them to 'stand back' and allow the children to make decisions for themselves.

We learned to stand back!

On occasions, children wondered 'how far' they could take an activity – building a tall tower of bricks for example, and adults had to learn not to interfere, preferring to speak to the children sensitively about consequences and responsibilities. Thus, children exercised greater judgement of when something was becoming too risky, and usually much further down the line than staff had previously experienced. As a result staff observed children growing in self-confidence (see Figure 4.5) Children became empowered to try out new ideas, move equipment and use it more inventively than before.

Figure 4.4 Examples of free-play activities

Activity	Description
Tower-blocks	Provide children with a range of construction blocks and allow them to make tall and elaborate structures. Be flexible in keeping the structures intact rather than tidying them away at the end of a session so as to ensure the children can 'finish' their work.
Big Clay	Provide a large amount of well-watered good-quality clay and allow children to help themselves to as much as they need. Keep tools away to encourage children to use their hands to manipulate the clay into whatever they like, either individually or in groups. Don't keep anything which is made – at the end of a session the clay is reduced to one big lump again – this ensures creativity in approach, rather than creations being precious (i.e. process rather than product is important here).
OHP	Provide children with access to an overhead projector and as many colourful and transparent objects as you can find. Allow them to move the objects round freely, making patterns on a large white wall or sheet. Observe both the children working *on* the OHP, and the children *reacting* to the projection (see Figure 4.2 and the book cover for images of this exercise).

Figure 4.5 Children enjoying free-play

Although much of the work was developed organically, upon reflection there were several elements that facilitated this growth.

Our approach became more thematic – and this was sometimes initiated by children. For instance, early in the project staff in one class had planned the theme of 'we're going on a bear hunt'. However, two days into the term, a group of children were digging outside and they were very excited about finding earthworms. Staff embraced this, and a significant amount of contextual work developed from this. The children made a wormery, they observed and drew the worms, they had worm stories, they made worms in clay and they wriggled like worms through tunnels. A bath was even filled with spaghetti and brown sauce, and pasta was made, cooked and eaten with gusto. As the term drew to a close, staff recognised that the children had moved on from the worms, and they felt more confident to observe and wait to see what the next 'theme' would be.

QUESTION FROM THE EDITOR

Consider the impact such approaches have upon the 'visibility' of children with special needs.

What might be the advantages and disadvantages of this approach?
On one hand, such children will participate more fully in activities, using their own strengths to engage with others and grow in confidence. It's important however, to stay alert to identifying areas of need for individual children and offer appropriate support where relevant. Read on to see how McMillan used digital photos to help with this aspect. . .

Alex, our creative practitioner became an integral part of the staff team. During debriefing meetings at the end of each day, which Alex also attended, children's experiences were discussed and strategies for the next day were planned. It took some time for the idea that our creative partnership should go beyond the days when Alex was here to take root. It also took time for the benefits of this way of working to reach classes other than those with which Alex was working.

It's important to consider how work with creative practitioners can be extended across the school. These issues were overcome for us by the desire of staff to instigate changes and a range of CPD experiences including:

- regular debriefing with all staff
- classroom experiments and feedback to other staff
- visits to other settings (including overseas) with reports to staff
- dissemination from conferences staff had attended.

It was crucial that staff were given the opportunity of seeing and experimenting with new and different ways of working. Every visit outside of the setting was reported to and discussed with all staff at weekly meetings, supported by looking at digital photos of these settings and examples of other people's planning.

We used digital cameras and ICT to help us 'stand back'. We had digital cameras in every classroom (and now every member of staff has one) and we used these in a variety of ways to support educational activities and display. For instance we projected images of the children's activities at home time for parents. More significantly, staff started using the cameras to document learning in a new way. Members of staff responsible for supporting children with special needs were experimenting with digital photography, using images to create 'Learning Journeys' as a method for documenting the play of the children.

When staff looked at images of one particular child at play, who had quite severe difficulties and very little verbal communication, we began to notice a pattern. Someone had captured a series of images of him putting different objects into a series of containers; another staff member had captured images of the child himself getting in, sitting in and looking out of boxes and play equipment; and finally someone had caught the moment when he led a member of staff to a large builder's bucket and indicated to her that he wanted her to get in it! Collecting these images together into a short and simple 'Learning Journey' helped staff members realise that the child's play was very inquisitive and focused on getting inside objects and exploring a range of different three-dimensional objects.

We also observed a boy who was experiencing social difficulties and undergoing assessment to determine whether he was on the autistic spectrum. He was fascinated by other children's play with sticks and objects. Previously, this would have been discouraged as being undesirable, partly because it could have been dangerous. In light of these experiences, staff recognised how this particular type of play was potentially helping his social development and interaction with other students, which didn't seem to occur in other activities, so was allowed to continue. This proved a wise decision as he established a role for himself, sometimes mimicking others, sometimes taking a lead and learning to stand up for himself. He confidently demonstrated his physical motor skills and was clearly very engaged.

These observations provided valuable information about the exploration and learning of individual children, which may not have been otherwise recognised and subsequently influenced the interactions we were able to have with them. The use of this medium provided both valuable learning but also encouraged members of staff to collaborate in ways they hadn't done before.

EDITOR'S COMMENT

Chapter 4 describes how Rosehill school set themselves a similar challenge – how do we make learning more visible?

We became much more attentive to classroom layout. The use of photographs alerted us to the possibility of seeing things differently, with new eyes. As a result, inhibitions were discarded and we started doing lots of crawling on hands and knees to fully appreciate the eye-view of our children. In light of this perspective, we took the opportunity to discard equipment which appeared too prescriptive (as well as too old or unattractive). Discussions followed about our outdoor spaces, the role of adult supervision and to what degree we could allow children greater freedom to explore and play. One decision taken was to allow children to choose the size of paper and materials they would use when drawing and painting and to make choices as to whether the floor or table was more suitable for their art making.

Overall, we became more conscious of the role of observation to inform learning in the future rather than assessment of learning in the past. We became more attentive to patterns in children's play, particularly with reference to their stage of development, the schema with which they were exploring and opportunities for further exploration and learning.

Key learning points

Staff came from a broadly 'child-centred' approach, with a belief in the importance of 'play' as the principal medium for learning of very young children. That said, the project required us to challenge our common practices and to develop a critical stance on the relationship between our structures, organisation, attitudes, interactions and individual children's learning. A key principle of our approach to exploring creative ways of developing a more inclusive and child-centred curriculum was the notion that: *children have expertise about their own learning.*

For us, this means children possess key knowledge about:

- what their individual interests are
- how they prefer to learn
- the ways in which they find it easier to express their understanding.

Our hypothesis was that the more we could recognise and understand these aspects, the more appropriately we could tailor the 'curriculum' for them and maximise their learning, rather than forcing them to follow a prescribed curriculum.

It was important for us to acknowledge the individual child as a learner, here and now, a 'being', rather than a 'becoming'. We challenged ourselves to see our children as already in possession of attributes to develop rather than with deficits, as often exposed by a fixed curriculum. Approaches developed through the project included:

- giving children greater freedom
- starting with the child's experience, personalised learning
- using visual documentation
- collating learning journeys
- staff collaborating to identify the 'next steps'.

These have all since become embedded in our everyday practice and systems. Children providing a lead in their own learning has become central to our approach.

EDITOR'S COMMENT

Mainstream and special education contexts advocate many advantages to personalised approaches to learning.

• What would count as an appropriate curriculum for pupils at your setting?
• What might be the advantages of a more personalised approach in your setting?
• What pitfalls would you anticipate and how could these be avoided?

How do you, and other staff members, feel about students taking the lead? Are there any issues you can identify in advance that would need to be resolved to maximise the success of a project like the one described in this chapter?

How does such a personalised approach contrast with a fixed curriculum or a competencies based approach similar to that described in Chapter 3?

What might be the merits and limitations of either, or a combination, in your context?

There were three particular factors which were instrumental in the success of our change journey.

1 The first factor was *time*. There was an existing and longstanding relationship with the creative practitioner, which meant new projects, ventures and directions did not start from scratch. Alex worked with the school for 2 days a week over 5 terms, which meant there was time to experiment, time to play, time to think and time to talk. By the end of the partnership, many of the changes to practice were embedded throughout the school.

2 The second factor was the *willingness and desire* of people at the school to embrace radical proposals and changes to practice. Change can be very threatening so staff needed to be confident enough in their practice to be able to explore new ideas, experiment and make changes with the full support of senior leadership.

3 The third factor is the nature and quality of the *relationship and partnership* between the school and the creative practitioner. A longstanding relationship encourages depth, ensuring that time is used to greatest effect. Mutual respect, trust and understanding were already well embedded, which meant that when there were issues, they could be resolved more easily.

EDITOR'S COMMENT

'Relationship' is a word frequently cited as critical to effective practice and partnership working but what does it mean and what does it entail? What defines a quality,

> creative and critical professional relationship to you? It's well worth agreeing how you want to work together at the outset.

What next?

The work at McMillan continues, with staff developing further ways of enhancing the experiences of our children and our engagement with parents. At the time of writing, we are developing a 'Forest Schools' programme of work, taking both children and parents into woodlands to explore learning in natural environments whilst working with parents at the same time.

The importance of meeting collaboratively to share and explore thinking is fully embedded in our practice, which means that together we encourage ongoing experimentation, responsible risk taking and pushing the boundaries. Opportunities are created for children and staff to engage with research projects together. Staff have learned to recognise the different 'lenses' through which they look at children's explorative play, which means they can ensure their reactions and responses to the children are personalised and focused on further learning.

Resources

Useful books

Cutler, A. (2005) *Signposting Creative Learning*, Kent, Creative Partnerships Kent. This contains useful models for conceptualising creative partnerships and their evaluation.

Katz, L. (2004) The challenges of the Reggio Emilia approach, in J. Hendrick (ed.) (2004) *Next Steps Toward Teaching the Reggio Way* (2nd edn), New Jersey, Prentice Hall. Can we 'do' Reggio? – Lilian Katz discusses the processes of change.

Moss, P. (2001). The otherness of Reggio, in L. Abbott and C. Nutbrown (eds) (2001) *Experiencing Reggio Emilia*, Buckingham, OUP. An interesting discussion on the philosophies of Reggio and how they translate into other educational settings.

Owen, N. (2010) Creative development, in I. Palaiologou (ed.), (2010) *The Early Years Foundation Stage – Theory & Practice*, London, Sage. Contains an intriguing take on creativity, and a creative partnership between a school and practitioner.

See also Rob Elkington's book, *Turning Pupils onto Learning: Creative Classrooms in Action*, which is also part of this series (Routledge, 2011). There are case study chapters from Lillian de Lissa and Leighswood Schools, which also engaged with the Reggio approach and Forest Schools.

Websites

http://www.reggioemiliaapproach.net/
Useful website, describing the approach and contains a network of interested pre-schools across Europe.

http://www.sightlines-initiative.com/
Sightlines organise visits to Reggio, as well as study tours to Denmark and Sweden. Their journal 'ReFocus' is full of contemporary research and ideas.

CPD ACTIVITY

This may be only a short exercise to describe but could lead to considerable insight and debate.

Consider how visits to other settings, particularly those with contrasting practices, may inform your own school development. An international visit may be expensive and take some time to organise but could be extremely illuminative, as it has been for McMillan. The British Council website (http://www.britishcouncil.org/school partnerships.htm) provides information about applying for funding to visit overseas partner schools as well as a selection of interesting case studies.

Consider how these practices will be documented. A visual record may help staff to see things differently. It may well be worth spending some time working on an observation framework, to identify priorities and contrast practice with your own context.

If such a venture is impractical, national possibilities may also be illuminating as well as easier to fund and arrange. Consider something like swapping classrooms or classes with another teacher, from your own or another school, as this will also encourage different perspectives. And if this isn't practical either, why not look at some case study research as a staff team, such as those in the ReFocus journal, suggested by Alex and Andrew.

In either case, think about how your findings will be reported to your colleagues and what may happen as a result.

Chapter 5

Working with creative partnerships

Mike Scott, Brays Special School, Birmingham

Editor's introduction

This chapter reflects on a partnership over several years between Brays Special School and Creative Partnerships (CP). It highlights how they have strived to enrich their curriculum for children at their school, so that they have far greater opportunity to participate in creative projects and develop their own creativity.

HOW TO USE THIS CHAPTER

One of the key themes from this chapter is *sustainability*. The learning shared offers clear advice about how to avoid the 'Show and Go' culture of short term arts-based projects in favour of structural change, resulting in protected time and space for children to explore and develop their creativity. As much of the reflection is about the nature of partnerships, this chapter will be interesting to any setting wishing to maximise long-term critical friendships that benefit school change.

The school context

Brays Special School is a small special school in a suburban area of Birmingham, with pupils coming from across the entire city. There are around 80 pupils on the roll at any one time, ranging from age 3 to 11. Classes are generally organised in age groups. With no grouping by ability, class teachers are presented with a very wide range of learning, physical, medical and complex difficulties in every lesson, even in a typical group of just eight pupils. Each class is supported by two or three permanent teaching assistants, who have played a key part in embedding the creative approaches shared in this chapter.

The challenge

As the introduction to this book alludes, any effective special education setting is a place of continuous innovation and creativity for many reasons. As children and young people present teachers with their personal, physical, sensory, communicational and learning needs, all of which can change quickly or imperceptibly over time, the challenge is always present to adapt the curriculum to enable the best possible access for every child.

As a result, those working with children experiencing serious difficulties have and continue to acquire and create hi- and low-tech approaches and tools for supporting their needs and enhancing their participation with the learning process. Despite working in an environment surrounded by the outputs of numerous creative ideas and processes, the staff at Brays have continued to challenge ourselves:

How can we continue to enrich the learning environment and experiences we provide for our students?

We have become engaged in a process of change, which has evolved over a period of five years and continues to do so. Our impetus was a desire to move beyond one-off arts-based events to something more long lasting. Hence another challenge focused upon:

How can changes we make be shared across the school and sustained over time?

No master plan was involved. In fact, it would have been counter productive to have been too prescriptive because we did not have the experience or knowledge, which have emerged since that time. In this chapter, we hope to share with you some of what we have learned.

Our timeline

2002   Oily Cart Theatre Visit
        Started work with Creative Partnerships
2003   'Excuses' storybook project.
        Estelle Morris MP attends book launch
2006   Work with Sarah Jenkinson
        Work with Peter Wynne Willson (Birmingham REP Theatre)
2009   Work with Harry Dawes

Starting point

In 2002, we were visited by The Oily Cart Theatre Company (see resource list), a vibrant and innovative group who devise interactive and multisensory drama for children with special needs. A show of theirs, called 'Boing!', involved assisting the physical movement of each child taking part whilst stimulating all the senses. It took place inside beautiful tents, the material of which was awash with various bright and colourful projections (see Figure 5.1).

Oily Cart's multisensory approach was a combination of many strategies which were already being used in the school on a smaller scale, but the success of the dramatic combination of visual and sound stimulation, delivered slowly and repetitively, demonstrated that we could benefit from exciting and stimulating learning experiences on a much bigger scale. To realise such an objective, we recognised the need for a new form of collaboration with creative practitioners.

Figure 5.1 Example of a workshop space

Creative Partnerships

Also during 2002, the school started working with CP. I was asked to be the coordinator of this project at our school, though I was not clear what this would involve during those early stages. In Birmingham, schools were encouraged to apply to be involved with CP as a cluster and in our case we did so along with two local mainstream primary schools, a secondary school and the Birmingham Hospital School. The cluster decided to work together as much as possible, sharing creative practitioners and projects when it was appropriate. Over the next three years we were able to organise annual events, when all of the schools worked together towards a large-scale celebratory event, bringing a welcome inclusive approach to the work overall.

For all of us involved at the beginning, it was very important that the first project was visible, exciting and, most of all, a success! That project was the making of a photograph-based story book, called 'Excuses', which combined 8–9-year-old pupils from our school with a group of pupils from Stanville Primary School. The project culminated with a book launch and the guest of honour was the Rt Hon Estelle Morris MP, the Education Secretary at the time, who had herself been instrumental in the conception of Creative Partnerships.

For the following two years, the projects with creative practitioners involved a range of teaching staff and classes, working with excellent dancers, artists, musicians and stained glass window specialists. Despite the projects being wonderful short-term experiences, we became aware they were not making as much impact on teaching and learning as they might have done. The development of creativity in these early stages, whilst being hugely enjoyable, was incidental and yet to be recognised for what it could contribute to whole-school change. We then asked ourselves: how could the enjoyment be converted into sustainable whole-school creativity?

Working together to stay open to possibilities

In this account, we learned that creative experiences for our children profited from:

- *collaboration* that brought together different people with different skills to offer our pupils new ways of engaging with arts-based activities
- remaining *flexible and open-ended*, so that projects could harness the resources of our pupils' existing creativity and the direction in which they wanted to take their creativity.

Our account starts in 2006, when we decided to have a common project across all of the schools in our cluster, involving art and outdoor classrooms. It involved Sarah Jenkinson, a visual artist (see resource list). After the visit of Oily Cart, we had been haunted by the sense that visual art remained difficult to teach to those same pupils who had benefited so much from the project, hence this informed our focus. At the same time, we were looking to create more teaching room by using outdoor spaces around the school.

Sarah used projection, materials, scrap items, tactile experiences and play. As these resources were readily available, we felt this was indeed something we could learn from and do ourselves. However, Sarah also devised with us a way of recording both the work being done and the process by which it was achieved. She left us with a beautiful book (see Figure 5.2), which was filled with photographs of golden moments. The book also had

Figure 5.2 The Grimble . . .

questions, comments and observations throughout. This document was very important. It gave permanence and validity to the work, which could be shared with others.

EDITOR'S COMMENT

How are creative skills captured and documented in your setting? Would Sarah's approach be helpful?

Also in 2006, I was asked to join a small group of teachers to work with The Birmingham Repertory Theatre on the commissioning of a new work for children. This ambitious project resulted in a play called 'The Shooky'. However, the most influential aspect of the project as far as Brays School was concerned was the appointment of Peter Wynne Willson as writer, and the relationship we were to develop with him.

His method of writing the story was to visit four schools, including Brays, to begin and develop the story line from pupils' own ideas. Yet, his work at Brays was quite a different experience for him as our children gave him unexpected responses. For instance, whilst holding up a piece of colourful material Peter asked what it might be (see Figure 5.3). He was told it was a rainbow with a thread hanging from it to make it possible to pull it to Earth. Unexpected and beautiful, it took the story into a new area for Peter to develop, but for us it was a reminder that our children have plentiful resources of creativity and imagination within them already.

What proved to be crucial for our school was a project that brought Sarah and Peter together, along with our experienced Exceptional Needs coordinator and a teaching assistant to face a much more open project than any of us had attempted before. It led to what was for us a ground-breaking partnership resulting in a novel approach we called 'sensory drama', which could be co-led by the pupils. There was to be no pre-defined product – this was about process. Instead, the project started with a research question: 'How can we enrich the teaching of drama and story-telling so that it is accessible to all pupils?'

Until then, it was the norm to have a story for the whole class, and to differentiate it for pupils who had sensory impairment and/or learning difficulties. Often, these attempts were misguided however as the support provided was somewhat tokenistic. As an example from my own personal experience, when telling the story of 'Peace At Last' by Jill Murphy, I found myself giving a fluffy hedgehog to a child in some vain hope that this would help her understand what I was talking about. It clearly did no such thing. As a school, we needed to challenge ourselves to think more carefully and critically about how we supported the creative learning of our pupils.

The collaboration between Sarah and Peter pulled together the multisensory elements we had identified, combining story and drama, outdoor spaces and a wide range of objects as stimulation. As Sarah noted in our evaluation:

> The project involved story-making, exploration, role-play, transforming outdoor areas, collecting, creating and responding to objects. Some particularly interesting objects used were those that had interesting sounds, or textures, those which were open to

Figure 5.3 What might this be?

interpretation or abstract, containers such as bags or boxes . . . objects with a sense of having had a life.

This approach removed several disadvantages for children who did not have prior knowledge about the properties of objects. The focus was on their sensory properties and the children's reactions to these. We use the term 'differentiating upwards' to describe this inclusive and collaborative way of working, with staff and children co-exploring and co-constructing new knowledge arising from children's initial experiences and interests.

EDITOR'S COMMENT

Can you think of any examples of 'tokenistic' practice? How could you reframe the activity so it is differentiated upwards?

Staying open to process is important when starting with children's experiences. It is so often the magical and unexpected moment in a lesson which makes the greatest impression and creates an opportunity for deeper learning or learning in a completely different direction. It is difficult to explore these opportunities when the curriculum is driven by its content. To make the most of such opportunities, we recognised the need to *pause, observe* and *reflect*.

A comment from our own evaluation underlines this importance:

> Crucial to the success of the process is the idea that, for this kind of work, there are no right answers. There are forms of open question and choice which lead to more interesting stories. The facilitators in these sessions need to free themselves from the pressure of always moving on, or always speaking.

Questioning thus became central to projects, and no project could begin without the research question being identified and agreed, which could then be used as a reference point. Having learned to explore new directions together, we remained aware of the need to embed opportunities for creativity into our school structures and systems.

Beyond 'show and go'

A skilful creative practitioner can be inspiring, but sometimes also daunting. Children are enthralled and produce great and diverse work, but staff can easily be left with a real feeling of inadequacy. 'I could never do that' is a common response, and so the result is an exciting event or project with no legacy. I call this 'show and go' when working with visiting practitioners, and it is something we try to avoid. Children, teachers, teaching assistants and practitioners all share the processes of planning, doing and evaluating. This helps ensure projects are feasible and well supported as well as disseminated across the school. However, such a shared process requires structures in place and opportunities for everyone's voice to be heard.

To help enable this to happen, an expanded teaching role was created for me. I was already teaching our class of 8–9-year-olds part of the week alongside a role as our music specialist, when I adopted a new role with the aim of integrating Music, Sensory Drama and Art, and to teach these subjects in half-day blocks in every class.

This created a two-tier input of creative teaching and learning within the school. On the one hand, Creative Partnerships continued to develop their projects and on the other hand, my new role involved transferring many of these new skills and ideas from CP projects into lessons. This proved to be an effective means of ensuring greater sustainability of new ideas and practices. Over time, all teaching assistants would become aware of developments even if their class had not participated in the CP project that had originally produced them.

EDITOR'S COMMENT

How could such a champion of creativity help embed pockets of effective creative practice in your setting?

Creative spaces

In 2009 we continued our exploration of sensory drama, this time with Harry Dawes, who began working with us on approaches to develop 'call and answer' activities, which are used to encourage communication. Arising from our initial work together, we came to realise that two important factors were affecting creative learning at Brays.

The first was the way our classrooms were set up, which emanated a great deal of 'visual noise' on the walls, and what might be clutter to some of our pupils. The notion of a magical space, which had been explored by Sarah and Pete in the sensory drama project, had not translated into classrooms.

Second, the day-to-day disturbances common to special schools, such as visits for medical and physiotherapy purposes, were accepted uncritically as necessary interruptions to be negotiated throughout the entire day. Hence, we discussed the notion of a 'golden time', free from any disturbance for twenty or thirty minutes. This, in turn, encouraged us to go further and dedicate a space to sensory drama, which could be used by groups. An area of the school previously, but infrequently, used for floor-based physical activity was transformed into a drama studio, where we can now build exciting and flexible sets which provide a multi-sensory stimulus for all pupils to learn about the themes they are studying.

Key learning points

Upon reflection of what we have managed to achieve so far in partnership, the following themes highlight some of our areas of learning.

Secure funding

The issue of funding for a small school can place the governing body, under the guidance of the head teacher, in a difficult position. Funds for resources, structural alterations and staffing obviously have to be found and approved, hence it is imperative to have support at this level. The fact that such a positive impetus was placed on creativity has been very important at our school.

Leadership

Embedding creativity into school life needs clear and supportive leadership. Innovation needs to be scrutinised. It is possible to make risks manageable by regular discussion and evaluation between the senior management team, the teachers and creative practitioners. Communication and a clear vision are essential, and we found that close reference to the school's improvement plan provided clarity for everyone involved, particularly as staff members enjoy frequent opportunities to contribute to this plan.

Long-term thinking and planning

The presentation to the pupils of exciting, well-resourced activities and learning spaces has been shaped by collaboration with creative practitioners who have actively engaged with the school's long-term aspirations and challenges.

It is important that creativity is ubiquitous, woven through the fabric of the curriculum, rather than the case where space is found here and there on the timetable, if and when possible.

Projects involving creative practitioners need time for planning and discussion. In a small school the issues around cover for teachers to have time for planning and evaluation with a practitioner can be onerous, so effective systems need to be found.

Collaboration with partners

Relationships with practitioners have identified several strategies for sustaining creative learning, including identifying a dissemination role for a teacher and dedicating physical and timetable space to creativity.

Our commitment to reflective practice has extended to close links with other establishments, including The Disability and Special Needs Inclusion Group based at the University of Birmingham. Such connections provided the school with further critical support as well as opportunities to engage with research and other ideas.

Defining and agreeing the nature of the relationship between CP

We have also looked closely at defining the essential characteristics of a successful collaboration with a practitioner. Carol Graham, a story teller who has come to know the school extremely well, has produced an extremely useful handbook called 'The Evolution of a Project' (see resource list), following her early work with us. With its diary form and questions, very much in Sarah Jenkinson's earlier style, it can be useful as a worthwhile training manual, or for a staff meeting which will provoke a great deal of useful discussion in any school setting.

Ownership

There is very limited benefit in one member of staff, or even a small number of staff, being enthused and enthralled by innovation, even if their teaching practice is changed for the better. For sustainable change, colleagues need to take ownership too. This may be aided by careful planning around key issues, such as ensuring the right practitioner works with the right class.

Reflection also needs to be shared. No project goes on behind closed doors or else its impact will, at best, stay in that room. Teachers here benefited from sharing the successes and setbacks of creative projects with each other in the spirit of supportive and critical friendship.

Anticipating challenge

Reflective practice is painful sometimes and it is quite possible that some people will find it more difficult than others to be self-critical, never mind have others pass comment on their work. However, this concern can often be addressed by an initial planning session that agrees a question/focus for the project. Regular, though brief, evaluation sessions can constantly bring events and thoughts back to this central question and depersonalise any issues; e.g. 'What did we agree to investigate, and how does what we have all done address that?'

Responding to setbacks

Whole-school change is made possible by learning from what goes wrong as much as what goes well. We have learned that it can be a bumpy road, and sometimes we feel as if we are being knocked off course but the overall momentum is undeniably forwards. This is where having a long-term but flexible commitment to change makes it easier to accept and learn from setbacks. Supportive evaluation is vital at such junctures.

Basic enabling skills

Creativity amongst children with additional difficulties needs to be built upon basic enabling skills – physical mobility, motor control and communication alongside behavioural support and other bespoke interventions that can make a crucial difference in terms of their inter-action with the wider world. Identifying pre-requisites to learning for individuals working towards personal targets is thus essential so they continue to develop these skills.

Taking time to pause, observe and reflect

Pupil learning may occur in small steps and be very subtle, so it is important to build in times to pause and observe their learning. Careful attention and reflection can lead to insight concerning the learning preferences of individuals, which in turn may inform a personalised approach to their curriculum. When children's needs prevent them from sharing as easily as other peers, careful observation may be a means to accessing their voice as their 'voice' can be communicated via subtle gestures.

Listening

Adults working with children need to prioritise listening. This is particularly important when working with children with special needs as their ideas may be unexpected and communicated in unfamiliar ways. Not everything will be practical but adults frequently need to take on the role of the advocate for their interests and wishes.

Positive feedback

Creative and carefully planned experiences can lead to pupils recognising their own creativity. To have such achievements noted, praised and developed further builds greater trust and security from which further creativity may develop.

What next?

For us, whole-school change will continue to involve the creative practitioners who have built up strong reciprocal relationships with us. That continuity has had a positive impact on our staff development, which we feel has been accelerated by focusing more effectively on specific areas for improvement. Trust continues to be key; talking, sharing stories and ideas, successes and setbacks, supporting each other and accepting the knocks have become vital to the whole process. Greater feelings of collective responsibility and job satisfaction will continue to be enhanced as a consequence.

The funding which has made these relationships possible will not go on forever, of course. It has therefore been important to plan projects carefully to end on time, having achieved what was intended, and for the changes achieved to be sustainable without exceptional financial support from outside the school budget. Once the expenditure on creative practitioners has to stop, or reduce, the changes or the tools for change have to be in place. If work remains to be done, the project should have left the school with the skills and knowledge to go it alone the rest of the way.

We share our experiences as widely as possible with schools who share the aspiration to invigorate teaching and learning, and intend to continue to learn through collaboration and research as to how we can continue to improve our practice. Our collaborations with creative practitioners, universities (including research students), pupils' families, businesses and the wider community will continue so that each can contribute to this aim. There will always be questions to be tackled and long may that continue.

Resources

Websites

http://www.oilycart.org.uk/
The company continues to pioneer innovative multi-sensory drama and tours new shows regularly.

http://www.storyspace.co.uk
The web site of Carol Graham, based in Hereford, who is mentioned in this chapter. She can provide INSET in storytelling and pupil voice which are both central to some aspects of creativity.

http://www.soundsofintent.org
The website of the 'Sounds of Intent' Project. The importance of pupils being able to express themselves, and be heard, has been mentioned in this chapter. This project is specifically relating to music, and the assessment of responses to music and sound. However, this inevitably involves PSHE and communication skills. Indeed, I know of schools which timetable music as 'communication'. For special schools it provides an alternative to P Levels, with realistic emphasis on achievement. I recommend visiting their website and looking at the assessment tool.

http://www.ted.com/talks/ken_robinson_says_schools_kill_creativity.html
A 20-minute video which all teachers should watch at least once. Ted.com also contains many other inspirational talks.

Book

'The Evolution of a Project' by Carol Graham
This book is not reproduced but is in our possession. A copy can be provided by contacting Mike Scott, Brays School, Brays Road, Sheldon, Birmingham B26 1NS. It will illustrate how a project with a creative practitioner might be planned and delivered, and how it might be recorded within school for colleagues to share.

CPD ACTIVITY

In supporting teacher confidence and competence in creative teaching the involvement of a creative practitioner is key. There are tales about artists who have visited schools where the collaboration has mis-fired, ended acrimoniously or simply not delivered what was expected. Yet, when managed carefully, the partnership can be a challenging but rewarding and enjoyable catalyst for change.

This activity is designed to make the collaboration enjoyable but also for the outcomes to include sustainable change for everyone involved – pupils, teachers, the creative practitioner and the school as a whole. A good experience shared is far more beneficial than one which affects only one member of staff.

The project I always wanted to do

The questions to be asked about a collaborative project include:

- What are we going to do?
- Can we sum up the work in an action research question, such as 'How can working with music technology improve pupil engagement and interaction in composition?'
- Why are we doing it?
- What will the end result look or feel like?
- What kind of artist or creative person will we need?
- Who else is going to be involved?
- How will we make sure it stays on track?
- Who is in overall charge?
- How will we know if it has been a success?
- How will we share the project with the rest of the school?

A School Improvement Plan (SIP), or similar, is one place where the vision of the school, the management team and governors is clearly set out, and the commitment (including financial) is made. Have it available and invite staff to have read through it in advance.

Task

- Select one improvement target from the plan relating to pupil achievement, perhaps in one year group or any other cohort within the school. Invent one if nothing leaps out.
- You have £3000 to spend.
- Discuss the questions above, in the order they appear.

The important universal issues in answering these questions tend to be:

- *Time.* Projects need time for planning and evaluation from the outset, and reflection at least at a mid-point and at the end.
- *Share the questions above.* The practitioner should know exactly why the school wants to do this work. Look at any plan together.
- *The action research question.* Constantly go back to the question you agreed at the beginning. Are we all still addressing it? This includes the pupils because their expectations of the project will be based on what they were told at the outset.
- *Success criteria.* If this project is about a *product* – a performance, an installation, a display etc. – make certain it is achievable on the budget, on time, and with everyone involved every step of the way. Having a product in mind can bring pressures into the collaboration as time runs out. If the product is about *process,* learning new skills and reaching for something innovative, the pressure is alleviated.
- *Control.* Final decisions have to be the teacher's. Democracy is important in maintaining involvement but this is about what the school requires. The action research question is based on that.
- *Sustainability.* Find an effective way to show others in the school the new skills acquired (by teachers as well as by pupils). A performance is one thing, but a diary of the project lasts a lot longer and is available to anyone who cares to inspect it, including in the future.

Chapter 6

Making learning visible

Wendy Johnson (Creative Agent) and
Andy Sloan (Deputy Headteacher),
Rosehill Special School, Nottingham

Editor's introduction

This chapter shares an interesting account about how Rosehill, a special school for children with autism, has attempted to balance opportunities for creativity with their students' needs for familiarity. Given that some of their students with autism have limited communication, it is difficult to always fully appreciate the nature and degree of learning taking place, even when it appears to be clearly happening. Inspired by this challenge, staff at Rosehill have worked with a range of creative practitioners to make learning more visible.

HOW TO USE THIS CHAPTER

This chapter has an assessment and planning focus. Not all children are able to clearly articulate what they have learned and this chapter will be useful to any professional interested in documenting learning that takes place in the absence of spoken language. It will also be useful to all those who work with children who demonstrate a broad range of ability across the whole curriculum, particularly creative subjects, which may be better served by more visual approaches to evidence capture.

The school context

Rosehill Special School, Nottingham caters for pupils on the autistic spectrum, aged from 5 to 19 years. The majority of pupils have severe autism but we also have learners from across the entire spectrum. Whilst we have some higher functioning students, many have little or no spoken language. In some respects, all of our teaching is creative as alternative forms of communication have to be frequently employed and adapted.

Pupils with autism also need clearly defined spaces and consistent routines in order to prevent anxiety. This presents a challenge to working spontaneously and/or creatively. For example, our students and teachers have experienced some difficulties in the past, when art therapists have altered the space and furniture in a room to undertake their activities.

Our work with Creative Partnerships, and as a School of Creativity, has thus focused on making the learning of this diverse group of pupils more visible and providing secure bases, which also allow our pupils opportunities for creativity.

The challenge

We feel that pupils at Rosehill School make significant progress whilst learning with us, particularly in areas of socialisation and communication. We have been moving away from traditional learning methods for some time now, preferring instead to give the pupils opportunities to use all of their senses to explore and understand the world around them. Creativity plays a key role. Their learning takes place not behind a desk but in all areas of the school environment, encouraging them to become more co-operative and investigative. However, currently much of the evidence we have to support our assessment of their learning is anecdotal. Hence we need to devise more appropriate recording procedures to deepen our understanding of how creativity impacts on teaching and learning in our school. Our challenge can thus be described as: how do we observe, record and capture vital moments of learning?

At the same time, our students need a very safe and predictable environment in order to feel relaxed and free from anxiety so that learning can take place. Clearly defined areas, clear routines and repetition need to play a big part in underpinning the creative approaches we use with our students. Therefore, a secondary challenge for us is: how do we create spaces that afford both security and opportunities for creativity?

In this chapter, we share the learning that has taken place whilst being involved with several projects with Creative Partnerships (CP), focusing particularly on these two issues.

Our timeline

2004	Work with Creative Partnerships starts.
2007	Creation of dedicated arts space, which became the MILE (Multisensory Interactive Learning Environment).
	Big Art project and a range of other projects, focusing on creativity across the curriculum.
2008	Creative Partnerships 'School of Creativity' status achieved.
	Audit of creativity in the school.
Jan 2009	School debated competencies curriculum and current recording systems.
May 2009	Video-based staff training (see text).
Jun 2009	Whole-school project, 'Africa', focusing in on observing creative teaching and learning and recognising competencies.
Nov 2009	Creation of a team focused on observation and reflective practice to enhance creative planning and curriculum development.
	New school building also starts.
May 2010	Research and training to explore observation, documentation and reflective practice happening in other settings, including staff training session with Emma Pace from Sight Lines.
July 2010	Staff team/ practitioners introduce frameworks for recording and reflecting on their own learning.

Starting point

Before beginning our work with CP we had already established links with many local creative outlets, including an art gallery, cinema and contemporary theatre. Professionals and students based at these locations had run successful events, workshops and projects with us. We were also beginning to establish links with Salamanda Tandem (see resource list), a company specialising in working with young students with autism through music and movement. Through the creative projects we had already experienced, members of staff had begun to identify the potential of creative activities for promoting learning for young people with autism.

We joined CP in 2004, keen to be involved with this forward thinking project. This relationship enabled the school to begin to organise and develop ideas around creative learning. One of the first initiatives was to transform a dilapidated classroom into a creative arts space. As pressure for space was at a premium, this decision was initially questioned but gradually staff recognised the value of this arts space and now as a new build is under construction, the first space included in the design was the area that has since become known as the MILE (Multisensory Interactive Learning Environment) (see Figure 6.1, p. 58).

MILE (Multi sensory Interactive Learning Environment) has a range of equipment that provides sensory learning scenarios. Staff are involved in a variety of training opportunities to support how they use the environment and link it to curriculum projects. Work in the MILE has focused on observing responses to different sensory stimuli. 'Intensive Interaction' (see resource list) is often used, which involves the young people deciding on the focus of their learning whilst adults provide support (see resource list for where to find more information).

From the outset of the project, the school recognised the need to build in sustainability. We wanted a lasting legacy of development rather than a range of big events that were exciting but had no lasting impact on children's learning. In order to achieve this, we incorporated the following points into our plan:

- We only used artists who were experienced at working with the needs of our students
- A large part of the initial work was dedicated to staff training
- Key staff undertook intensive training and provided support to colleagues
- Our first project, 'Big Art', worked with all the classes within the school over a period of two years.

This initial work formed an excellent baseline for future development. It was important in dealing with our second challenge, to provide security at the same time as opportunity for creativity, that we integrated creative times and spaces into our existing structures (see Figure 6.2, p. 59).

Big Art enables pupils to work on large-scale art projects using a range of materials, in both 2D and 3D. Projects utilise creative processes to help pupils explore and investigate links to other areas of the curriculum.

Figure 6.1 Images of children interacting with MILE after the classroom transformation

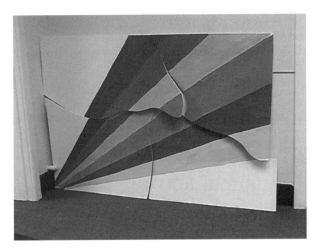

Figure 6.2 'Big Art'

Making learning visible

At our school, communicating with young people about the development of their learning can be problematic. We cannot use many of the basic strategies common to mainstream schools, including spoken language in some cases. However, some learners are able to express their views through:

- sign language
- symbols
- photographs, and/or
- social stories (the visual representation of various scenarios).

In other cases, staff need to be sensitive to *non-verbal* cues. A functional assessment of such things as body language and behavioural patterns may indicate that a learner is content or anxious about particular situations, environments or people. For some students, their behaviour is their principal form of communication.

Such factors make assessment of learning extremely challenging. To respond to this challenge, we wanted to learn more about how creativity specifically impacts on learning and we wanted our pupils' creative learning to be made 'visible', by which we meant we wanted to be able to observe and document things that we often don't notice or are easily missed or forgotten. We wanted to recognise creative behaviours at a deeper level. Having established this clear vision amongst the staff, we anticipated being in a better position to share our findings with other schools, colleagues and visitors.

It is not always easy to see learning in autistic pupils; learning may only show itself with a hand movement, a gesture, a noise or a moment's eye contact. So, we recognised the need to develop skills in observing, noting and responding to these often very tiny pieces of evidence which may well turn out to be a key element in planning an activity to stimulate further progression.

Case study

Figure 6.3 shows an example of an observation of a child exploring their environment inquisitively, which could be followed up with a range of creative classroom activities, including:

- using ribbons tied to the branches of a tree to observe how the wind moves them
- piling leaves on a large sheet of plastic, encouraging a group of children to bounce the sheet in the air to watch how the leaves move
- throwing buckets of small torn pieces of tissue paper into the air
- observing feathers and chiffon scarves floating in the air
- making kites using plastic carrier bags or paper and string
- making links to sensory body work, such as children experiencing their own body falling onto a mattress or pile of cushions.

EDITOR'S COMMENT

Consider how free exploration may reveal learning that may have gone unnoticed in your school and how this could inform the subsequent design of educational activities. Chapter 2 also deals with some similar issues, which may be of interest to you.

Linking back to the curriculum

Members of staff tend to observe pupils' responses and behaviour quite naturally but are more aware of the need to record their observations in relation to core subjects and basic skills as this is where present systems have greatest emphasis. This realisation led us to

Staff sit at a distance, allowing the pupil to explore fallen leaves during a trip to the nearby orchard. In this photograph the pupil seems to notice the leaf fluttering down, his face clearly shows that he is engaged. A member of staff has captured this moment and now they need to think about what happens next and how they can build on this interest. Collaboration with creative practitioners and other teachers may help to develop follow-on activities.

Figure 6.3 Exploring falling leaves

question the type and quality of information we use to inform and plan the development of our curriculum for autistic pupils. Throughout our work with CP, practitioners and individual staff have practised observing and recording in different ways but this documentation of pupil learning has generally stayed with individual profiles and has not been used in formal assessments of pupils or curriculum planning.

We were then eager to develop a school ethos with more reflective practice at its centre, alongside greater confidence with using a broader range of evidence to support observations of learning. We also felt this process would be better aided by moving away from a subject-based curriculum to a curriculum that reflected the key areas of learning for young people with autism. We embarked on a journey to identify what these areas might be and are now working towards identifying a set of key competencies (see Figure 6.4).

Figure 6.4 A competency-based curriculum for students with autism

Communication	Social Awareness	Thinking
Sensory Modulation	Organisational Skills	Behaviour Management

We were particularly keen to explore how these competencies could be developed through creative approaches, using a whole-school shared topic. We started and continue to discuss how to link curriculum design to ongoing observation of pupils' learning experiences and interests, with the use of video proving to be particularly helpful to the observation process (see Figure 6.5).

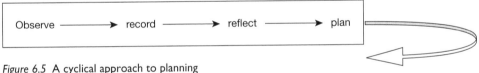

Figure 6.5 A cyclical approach to planning

Using video

We decided to carry out some investigative work with a dual purpose, i) to explore a curriculum based on competencies and ii) to explore new ways of observing and documenting learning so that we could plan a more appropriate curriculum for our students. We initially invited arts practitioners Amy Nicholson and Betti Copperwood (both with considerable experience of working with autistic pupils) to work with two classes. These sessions were recorded by a professional filmmaker (Tom Walsh), and we used the resulting film as a resource at a whole-school training day (see Figure 6.6).

The footage was intended to capture both when learning was and was not taking place, enabling staff and practitioners to reflect on an activity, its impact and aspects that were either stimulating or hindering learning. At our training day, we revisited our key challenge, linking it to curriculum change: how can we make learning visible and use it to inform our teaching and learning?

We also invited Mathilda Joubert (a consultant, researcher and trainer in creativity, innovation and the management of change) and Cynthia Pitts (Deputy Head Teacher at Fosse Way School, Bath) to facilitate the day for us.

Figure 6.6 Video still of students working together

For us, the advantages of inviting 'outsiders' to help us critique our practice were:

- To share our practice with others, seeing where there are synergies and where we can learn from experiences of others.
- To engage with 'experts in the field' to challenge our practice and goals.
- To motivate and inspire the whole school.
- To bring new perspective to our aspirations.

Prior discussions were held between the practitioners and the filmmaker, so they could create a manageable resource showing examples of Rosehill pupils taking part in creative activities.

The aims of the training were to:

- Provoke thinking and practice around observation, documentation and reflection.
- Help staff further develop collaboration skills to co-plan, co-teach and embed observation, documentation and reflection throughout their practice.
- Encourage and inspire creative approaches to develop the competencies identified by the school.
- Develop reflection on the teaching and learning happening throughout the project, informing future contexts for learning within the new curriculum.

The day was an inspirational stimulus, noteworthy for the following key outcomes:

- Opening dialogue around current practice and reflecting on areas for development.
- Helping staff to make connections in their practice.

- Driving aspirations for more clarity and direction in what we are trying to achieve.
- An increased perspective on the 'bigger picture'.
- Increased enthusiasm resulting in staff getting 'fired up' with a positive 'can do attitude'.

For many staff, this was the beginning of a journey into deeply reflective practice, whereby such detailed observations would inform future planning cycles of a competence-based curriculum. Staff also reflected on how they currently used observation and where they would now need further support.

Soon after, the whole school embarked on a shared project with 'MUNDI' (a Nottingham based Global Education and Citizenship Centre) on the topic of Africa. This provided us with an early opportunity to implement some of the principles and strategies earmarked during the training day. The project had a high status within the school, which created real excitement. Activity transcended classrooms, the playground and the MILE as well as the local orchard. Staff, students, parents and any visitor to the school would see, smell and hear evidence of the Africa project happening.

The intensive nature of the project challenged our school's routines and use of space as well as stimulating interesting discussion concerning the practicalities, planning and staff skills necessary to conduct deep observation. We will share what our key learning points were in the next section.

Key learning points

Our enquiry has become more focused over time, leading us to concentrate on the development of a competencies-based curriculum, which is enhanced by improving our skills of observation, documentation and reflective practice. This remains the main priority for us as we anticipate that improvements in the area of observation will inform continued refinement of the curriculum.

Since our involvement with Creative Partnerships and becoming a Creative Partnerships' School of Creativity more recently, all senior teachers have been supportive and fully involved in the movement towards a fully integrated creative curriculum and more labour intensive approaches to assessment and planning. This support is very important. For example it is much easier to alter the structures or timetable of the school, to release staff to discuss planning and evaluation together as well as deal with unanticipated obstacles swiftly when the programme has the full backing of all senior teachers.

However, we have experienced that observing, recording and documenting competencies effectively has been more onerous (see Figure 6.7) than expected and we have identified that we need to work with practitioners with specific skills to address challenges in these areas. Our most urgent challenge is to find manageable ways of incorporating deeper observation into everyday practice.

We have learned so far that such processes are supported by providing opportunities for staff to share their observations, plan and reflect together, thus encouraging staff to develop and embed pedagogical approaches unique to their groups.

Figure 6.7a Ways of incorporating deeper observation into practice and challenges

Tips for incorporating deeper observation into practice	Challenges that may need to be overcome
Work in teaching pairs or staff teams, where colleagues observe and note take. Ensure that time is allocated to discuss these observations.	**It is difficult to record everything that may be relevant** – focus will be needed. Work in pairs or staff teams to decide which pupil you are focussing on, what you have noticed beforehand and what you are looking for. **Finding time to discuss observation is often overlooked or time is difficult to find** – dialogue is essential for any meaningful impact. Allocate regular but achievable time slots specifically to discuss observations of pupils and how the learning of this pupil can move forward.
Set a cycle of challenges as a whole school to embed practices of observation and reflective practice together – at Rosehill, staff bring observations to staff meetings. Time is allocated to discuss the observations in groups, staff then use these discussions to help them plan how they can use them to support their planning, they then reflect with the group at the next meeting, which encourages a cycle of dialogue and shared planning.	**It is easy to miss out important elements of the cycle – or set unrealistic challenges** – encourage actions that have a focus and are manageable and always encourage support and sharing of ideas amongst staff.
Encourage students and staff to keep scrapbooks or e-portfolios (see CPD exercise).	**Time needs to be allocated and value given to the activity as part of the session.** This activity can become part of a routine – avoid getting too regimented about pupils' contributions though – use fresh approaches and new stimuli to challenge how pupils input and use journals. Creative practitioners may well be able to work with staff to introduce stimuli for journals.
If the opportunity allows, incorporate observation windows and opportunities for free exploration into classrooms.	**Observing learning can feel obtrusive for pupils and staff** – building a good dialogue and understanding of how observations are used will support staff to develop effective methods that don't disrupt teaching and learning in sessions. Observation windows can be effective but there needs to be respectful use of these to ensure staff are comfortable.
Capture a series of photographic stills of a pupil engaged in an activity. Add narrative to the images. Use the stills as a tool for discussion with other staff.	**Still photos can be interpreted in many different ways** – the knowledge of the pupils, the context, the journey and the different viewpoints of the people involved in the session are important, giving a more accurate account. We can never be fully sure that what we each see is accurate – narrative can certainly provide a more informed interpretation as an effective tool to plan for progression and as a source of evidence.

Figure 6.7a Continued

Tips for incorporating deeper observation into practice	Challenges that may need to be overcome
Share some selected video footage together in staff meetings – at Rosehill staff are asked to focus on one child, they then get into groups to discuss what they see.	**Staff may interpret things differently** – practising dialogue is therefore important, staff will then become more practised at considering the range of interpretations and pulling out areas they need to explore more closely. **Deciding what we are looking for** – video can be selected with a specific purpose in mind. For example, at Rosehill we are focusing on work with creative practitioners; this is helping staff to recognise creative behaviours and will support the development of a more creative curriculum.

Figure 6.7b An example of a set of photos taken over a short time frame with narrative added as a record of what is happening and how the pupil responds

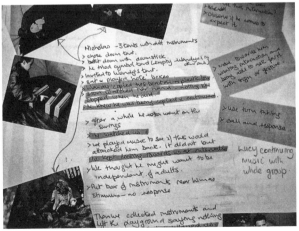

Figure 6.7c Observation and documentation of a session with a creative practitioner. Comments are highlighted to show an observation of behaviour alongside possible areas to develop on sticky notes

What next?

Developing observation skills and creative curriculum

Creative Practitioners and a small group of staff are continuing to work together to develop and improve existing structures and frameworks so they can work specifically for Rosehill School.

The relationship is focusing upon:

- developing and practising new skills around observation and reflection, which will become key to planning and delivery;
- supporting and enthusing staff to develop our understanding of creative learning, whilst also developing some specific creative tools to help them plan a creative curriculum.

The work will focus on two particular classes to enable greater depth of analysis as well as consistency for pupils who need that stability. Senior teachers are encouraging staff involved to take a leading role in cascading their learning across the school so that our practices and curriculum continue to be informed by this work.

We are also in the process of identifying and working with other external partners to explore educational philosophies that prioritise learning through exploration and discovery that encourage pupils to own and lead their own learning, such as through Intensive Interaction (see resource list) and/or Reggio practice (as described in Chapter 2).

During the next two years we hope to find out the following:

1   What systems can be put in place to ensure we are monitoring progression to inform a more creative curriculum, which is relevant and meaningful to pupils with autism?
2   How can working with practitioners support staff in creating opportunities for creative teaching and learning which is pupil led?

Informing our new school building

We are also in a very exciting phase of development at the moment as our school is to be rebuilt over the next year (through the 'Building Schools for the Future' fund). Our past and current work with Creative Partnerships is supporting the development of teaching and learning that will happen in our new building. As a result of this work, each class will have its own outdoor play area as an additional teaching space. We have planned that each classroom suite will have an observation window, which will allow a less intrusive presence when observing activities yet providing opportunities for staff to share and learn from each other, without distracting the pupils.

Resources

Article on Building Schools For The Future at Rosehill: www.independent.co.uk/.../pound8m-nottingham-redesign-will-create-an-environment-where-autistic-pupils-feel-safe-1895256.html

Artist and project related websites featured in the chapter

Mathilda Joubert: http://www.softnotes.com
MUNDI: http://www.mundi.org.uk
Salamanda Tandem: http://www.salamanda-tandem.org
SightLines – includes information about Reggio Emilia: http://www.sightlines-initiative.com/
Claire Simpson: http://www.somecuriousfinds.org.uk

Information and videos about Intensive Interaction

http://www.davehewett.com/index.php

CPD ACTIVITIES

Consider working with video to introduce observation and documentation to all staff as a way of informing forward planning and reflective practice. Ideally employ a professional filmmaker or skilled member of staff to video and edit pupils engaged in a range of school activities. It is important the filmmaker understands the intended use of the video. Video captures elusive moments of learning, which can inform fruitful discussion.

Or alternatively, why not consider introducing filming into regular classroom routines. There are now a range of affordable digital video recorders, many of which can also easily be used by children.

There are also a number of free or low-cost websites allowing individuals and groups to upload and share footage within a secure virtual space that has access restricted to those involved with the project. They also allow group members to interact and comment on each other's photos and videos. Such sites could be used in a number of ways:

- as a way of building individual e-portfolios for students
- as reminders to students of previous activities or as stimuli for lessons, or
- as stimuli to discuss with colleagues or other schools.

Consider how such sites may be helpful to collecting and sharing visual evidence about educational activities.

Also consider carefully any ethical issues that need to be resolved before piloting such approaches.

Chapter 7

Engaging Deaf students through ICT

Soren Hawes, Danuta Wdziekonska-Piwko, Katie Martin, Jane Thomas and Jon Nicholls, The Deaf Support Centre at Thomas Tallis School, London

Editor's introduction

This chapter shows how a number of ICT projects have been employed at Thomas Tallis School to:

- give students greater opportunity to demonstrate their learning via a form of communication with which they are comfortable
- afford Deaf students a more active role in the learning process, and thus
- develop greater independence and confidence.

The chapter contains two case studies showing how ICT has benefited individuals directly and signposts a number of challenges for professional development.

HOW TO USE THIS CHAPTER

Rather than describing a single project, what follows is the story of a series of inter-related initiatives that are ongoing and the lessons learned along the way. Although this chapter focuses on Deaf students, the insights are relevant for all schools, particularly those working with students whose additional difficulties obstruct demonstration of their learning via such traditional approaches as writing. These lessons are also applicable to students whose strengths are located beyond that of the core curriculum and its formal assessment. This is particularly pertinent in light of the case studies in this chapter, showing how the form of learning assessment greatly affects students' views of themselves and their learning. The ethical implications of this observation may warrant some discussion and either of the case studies make a suitable stimulus for a professional development event.

The school context

Thomas Tallis School is a Specialist Visual Arts College (1998–), situated in south-east London and serving a diverse community. There are currently a total of 1636 pupils on roll, including 443 students following post-16 courses. We have a significant SEN cohort at our school, which has climbed over recent years to its current level of about 30 per cent of the total school population. We have two Dedicated Specialist Provision units; one for students who are deaf or hearing impaired and one for students with speech and communication difficulties.

The new school building, part of the Building Schools for the Future project, has been designed to be a creative hub for the local community with a range of specialist resources. The school's specialist arts college status and its longstanding involvement with Creative Partnerships have accompanied a change process placing creativity at the centre of our school experience.

We believe that creativity lies at the heart of a 21st century education. In 2007 the school became one of thirty national Schools of Creativity. This achievement was built on recognition of the need to get students involved in action research. The Creative Tallis Action Research Group, a mix of students and members of staff, used a blog (see resource list) to document this research and promote discussions about creative learning. The group members quickly discovered a shared interest in new technologies, specifically Web 2.0 tools and online learning. A new website (see resource list) was created to:

- describe what we felt constituted a pedagogy for creative learning
- document successful learning and teaching strategies
- promote the use of web resources.

The adoption of new technologies to support creative learning has influenced practice across the school but has had the most profound impact in the Deaf Support Centre.

The Deaf Support Centre

The Deaf Support Centre was set up in 1997 to provide a mainstream context for young Deaf people with a range of needs. Before the centre was in place many students faced long journeys to schools outside of the borough or did not have access to comparable provision at all. The centre has between 15 and 20 students aged between 11 and 16. The students are not a homogenous cohort and have a complex range of needs and communications strategies (see Figure 7.1).

The needs of Deaf students

Deaf students can face particular challenges in accessing the curriculum taught in a mainstream school. Ninety-five per cent of Deaf students are born into hearing families and,

Figure 7.1 Students' needs at the Deaf centre

Some students might have a moderate or mild hearing loss and might access the curriculum with hearing aids and might use their voice to communicate with others	Some students might be cochlear implant users and might use a combination of speech and sign	Some students might have a profound or severe hearing loss and might access the curriculum through British Sign Language and use sign to communicate with others

Several students from these groups have other needs that might include a diagnosed language disorder, needs relating to autistic spectrum disorder, or additional complexities brought about by English not being the language spoken at home.

as a result, these children can face a challenge in developing age-appropriate language and literacy. The hearing child will have access to all sorts of passive learning and will have the ability as a young child to attend to an object whilst hearing its name, whereas a Deaf student is more likely to require knowledge and language to be explicitly taught in a way that addresses their particular communication needs. This, and other factors, often lead to students within the Deaf Support Centre having reading ages significantly below the level otherwise expected for their age, which presents challenges for fully accessing the curriculum.

The cognitive and linguistic elements of learning are so intertwined that a lack of early language often has an impact on the Deaf child's ability to acquire and retain new concepts and vocabulary. Those students for whom BSL is their first language face the additional challenge of, in effect, the curriculum being delivered in a second language. BSL, as a visio-spatial language, has no written equivalent and its grammar does not follow the grammatical or syntactical conventions of written or spoken English.

The challenge

At a Deaf Support Centre like the one at Thomas Tallis School, we encounter several challenges.

> *How do we recognise and harness the understanding and learning clearly taking place in British Sign Language (BSL) – learning which often cannot be expressed through conventional ways such as writing and reading?*

Many Deaf students have a good understanding of the concepts they are studying when operating in BSL, which is often best regarded as their first language. We were keen to find a way of making the best use of this ability, to investigate ways of creating resources that acknowledged their preferred mode of communication, and also discover ways of allowing them to communicate their understanding in the language with which they felt most confident and competent. As you will read, this has been aided by technologies such as film making and other new media becoming easier to use, more accessible and affordable.

> *How do we support our students to become more independent, engaged and creative?*

When our students are presented with a curriculum they often experience as extremely challenging, students can become rather passive and over-reliant on the in-class support they receive. We wanted to explore ways that allowed our students to use their own initiative, make decisions, use their judgement and to take greater ownership of their learning.

> *How do we help students feel better about themselves and their learning?*

We wanted to support our students to feel more confident, taking pride in the outcomes of their efforts and be more enthusiastic about learning. We were acutely aware that traditional forms of teaching and assessment often resulted in feelings of helplessness and diffidence in our students and wondered what effect alternative approaches may have on students' confidence and independence.

Our timeline

1997 Deaf Centre established
1998 School established as a Visual Arts College
2002 Started working with Creative Partnerships
      New school built
      Creative Tallis Action Researchers project started
2006 Life & Deaf produced
2007 Creative Partnerships 'School of Creativity' status achieved

Starting point – Life & Deaf

Following several small-scale projects with visiting creative practitioners that featured in the school's summer arts festival, two colleagues planned a more ambitious programme focused on creative writing. The output of this process was 'Life & Deaf', the title of a book and DVD created by Deaf students in October 2006. It started as a speech and language therapy project, which aimed to develop Deaf children's self-esteem and communication in signed, spoken and written languages. What started as a paper-based project came to life when the children engaged with technology. Film-making facilities allowed the students to capture signing and produce the first ever collection of children's poetry in BSL. The children actively engaged with photographers, film-makers and editors, allowing them to develop their ICT skills, whilst experiencing the creative world of work.

'Life & Deaf' afforded an interaction between low and high tech media. The children used paper and pens to draw designs which were scanned and developed using computer design technology. In a meeting of old and new worlds, the children performed their poetry to a live audience one evening and by the next morning, parents, professionals and students could download a podcast of the performance from the Thomas Tallis website. During the launch, projections of the children signing ran alongside printed posters in the exhibition space.

The DVD was widely distributed and took the reach of the project way beyond the potential of a printed poetry book. For Deaf students who struggle with literacy, the DVD allowed them to access poetry in sign language, whilst the use of subtitles made it accessible to all. The DVD was seen by a diverse range of audiences from viewers of the BBC's 'See Hear' to patrons of the bar in the Institute of Contemporary Arts, London. Following the success of this project, the 'Life & Deaf' website was created, which features free down-loadable materials for other schools and organisations to replicate the project. Poetry from all over the UK continues to be submitted and showcased on the website and we have received feedback from Deaf students across the country who use the site to read about the experiences of other Deaf children.

The success of this project brought into focus the challenges of 'how do we give students the opportunity to demonstrate their learning via their preferred method of communication' and 'how do we encourage them to be more independent', as previously introduced. In order to investigate how we might go about this, and encouraged by the experiment of 'Life & Deaf', we decided to investigate how we could use new technologies to better support this cohort of students.

A group of three students in a Geography class for 13–14-year-olds had become very interested in the topic of deforestation and had developed a very good understanding of the key concepts and ideas. As the topic was coming to an end, students were asked to write an essay explaining their understanding of the causes and consequences of deforestation. Although our Deaf students had a good understanding of the topic, they did not have the skills in written language to fully express what they knew, but they were keen to communicate their understanding in a more intuitive, and for them, enabling way. Their class teacher was very supportive and in collaboration with their communication support worker, they arranged for our Deaf students to sign their essay rather than write it. It proved to be a Eureka moment and students produced a signed essay which communicated a very thorough understanding of the topic and received an assessment level that matched or exceeded most of their hearing peers.

EDITOR'S QUESTION/CPD FOCUS

What alternative means of assessment may suit students at your school who find it difficult to express themselves in written forms?

An additional benefit was derived from the liaison with the Speech and Language Therapy team that were working with the same group of students to develop their communicative competence and their confidence in using speech. The students had been working with a technique called Cued Articulation (see book by Passy in our list of resources), where hand shapes and gestures are used to help students produce the phonological elements of speech.

As a result of not being able to hear their voices accurately, Deaf children do not get the aural feedback that helps them understand when a word is produced accurately. This can mean that students are reluctant to use their voices for fear of 'getting it wrong'. The same group of students were working on producing a film demonstrating the impact of cued articulation and they were now in a position to put together these two projects to develop their learning and communicative competence.

These projects gave us plenty of evidence of the learning benefits of using new technologies and acted as the stimulus for employing these strategies more widely amongst our students. Two case studies now follow showing how technology has been used to support our students.

Case study 1: Richard and short-film making

In the early stages of exploring how technology could support our Deaf students, we decided to focus our attention on a small group so we could understand the processes involved more intricately. This case study focuses on one student, Richard, and the impact of the use of new technologies on his progress between 14–16 years of age. Like many of our students, Richard had found it hard to access the mainstream curriculum as a result of his low reading age and literacy difficulties. He had started to become disaffected with the education on offer and had begun to recognise that the written work he produced was often inferior to the work produced by his peers. The impact of this recognition had led him to be rather passive and reliant on the support that he received in the classroom. That said, the staff that worked with him often noted that when given an opportunity to communicate his understanding through sign he was a much more keen and motivated learner.

We were eager to find ways of helping Richard become an active learner who was interested in planning and shaping his own learning, and also to find ways of encouraging him to make creative choices and decisions. To assess what impact access to new technologies might have upon his approach to learning we decided to give him the opportunity to produce a film as a formal piece of assessed coursework based on China's one-child policy.

Richard approached this in the following way:

- he decided to use images from the Internet and film footage from YouTube as the backdrop to his signed essay
- working with two other Deaf students in the class, they would sign their response to the essay question
- using a green screen, they would then superimpose themselves on images that related to the content of their work
- working closely with their communication support worker they then took on the additional responsibility of subtitling their film.

This meant that in effect they had produced a written response, but their first response was in a format with which they felt at ease. This allowed them to:

- communicate intuitively and effectively
- validate both their topic knowledge and skills in using BSL
- demonstrate the depth and scope of their understanding.

This also meant that by the time they started working with written English they were already very familiar with the topic and its key concepts and were far more willing to work on acquiring key vocabulary and developing the accuracy of their written English subtitles.

This approach allowed them to produce a film that impressed their peers and mainstream teachers alike. It meant that a task that would have been far more teacher led and supported by staff was much more student-initiated and saw Richard take far more responsibility for and interest in his work than would otherwise have been the case. Perhaps most significantly of all he was immensely proud of his efforts.

Building on the positive experiences so far we then put some thought into how we could offer a curriculum that would allow Richard to develop and build on the skills he had already acquired, and that would also allow him to develop further as an independent learner. We were fortunate that we could offer two appropriate vocational courses. The first was a practical Media course (accredited by BTEC) and the second was a course that accredits personal effectiveness (awarded by ASDAN). Two important features of both courses were:

- the opportunity to create tasks that invited Richard to take a keen and controlling interest in his work
- the inclusion of a flexible approach to assessment so that he was not being purely measured by what he could write.

Within the BTEC Media course, Richard has worked on a range of units including film making, photography and web authoring. Each unit has allowed Richard to create products that he is passionate about planning, developing and evaluating. He is now more engaged and determined to make his own decisions and develop his own ideas and projects. He had become a far more active learner!

In addition to the pleasure he took in the products that he made, he also developed a range of very marketable and '21st-century skills' such as film making, desk top publishing, web authoring and photography. A final significant gain from the course was the way in which the processes and products could be referred to and archived in Richard's ePortfolio (see resource list). His previous written work tended to be incomplete or required significant alterations and corrections, something which also caused Richard dissatisfaction.

His ePortfolio however, could be a selling point for both him and his school work. It had become a proud statement of his achievements and progress, informing a much more positive picture of his own identity as a learner. Richard's success and interest in media allowed him to take up a two-week work placement at Remark! – an editing house that provide subtitles and in-vision signing for a wide range of media. Not only did Richard have the chance to demonstrate and further develop his film editing skills, he was also working in a company that was led and run by Deaf adults. This provided him with a sense of what it might be possible for him to do and achieve later in life, as well as bolstering his confidence in his Deaf identity.

The ASDAN COPE Award is based around a series of challenges that, when handled creatively, allow students to choose tasks that they are interested in and allows them to represent their work, learning and progress in a very professional and eye-catching way. The students were allowed to use Mac laptops throughout the course and this helped them collate a range of materials that look incredibly professional. The programmes they used allowed them to revise, improve, edit and develop their work. Often paper-based tasks left the students rather frustrated by the number of errors they might have made; the ICT equivalent allowed them to make improvements without becoming disenchanted by crossings out, teacher corrections and multiple drafts.

It is also worth noting that many of the Deaf students were becoming more adept at developing approximate spellings of words that when typed could often be corrected by spell-check. Many of the communication support workers in the classrooms experience students asking them to laboriously finger spell words because the students are anxious to write them down accurately, and are reluctant to attempt to spell the words themselves for fear of making mistakes. When working on the computer they are much more willing to attempt to write independently, edit their work and take responsibility for addressing those words that the computer helps them recognise as being misspelt. The use of desktop publishing programs like Pages and presentation software like Keynote has also allowed them to take great pride in their ability to generate pieces of work anyone would be proud of. This has had a transformative impact on their self-concept and confidence.

Case study 2: supporting transition for Alex

The next case study focuses on an 11-year-old student who has recently transferred from primary to secondary school and demonstrates how the technology available in the Deaf Support Centre at Thomas Tallis School has played a vital role in assisting the difficult transition of Deaf students from primary to a secondary school.

Figure 7.2 Composite image of students using video, Comic Life and a blog to support their learning

The technology we have explored has helped students to overcome psychological barriers to learning based on previously experienced failures. This is well illustrated by Alex, a student with a moderate/severe hearing loss and a significant language disorder. Alex is a delightful, sociable boy who loves interacting with his peers but his motivation disappears as soon as he is put in a classroom environment and presented with a written task to complete. Alex experiences difficulties with spelling despite being very meticulous. He seeks perfection but is confronted by a sense of failure when traditional teaching methods are used, given the severe nature of his language disorder. Alex tends to withdraw; often without first trying when he knows that he cannot deliver work comparable to that of his peers. He will not ask for help as this will draw attention to his difficulties; instead he will employ a range of avoidance strategies and seek to distract others. We tried different strategies with Alex based on positive encouragement, but given the seeming incompatibility between what he is required to do and his ability to do it independently, these strategies were unsuccessful.

However, the picture was very different when Alex was given the opportunity to use ICT to help him access the curriculum. In their Learning Support lesson, Year 7 students were asked to write a short story about their autumn half-term holiday. After spending 15 minutes on producing one written sentence Alex was asked instead to send an email to the teacher explaining what he did during half term. He adopted an utterly different approach

WHY TRANSITION IS A PARTICULAR ISSUE FOR DEAF STUDENTS

Many Deaf students spend the majority of their time in small support units whilst at primary school and they are often only integrated into the mainstream setting for around 20 per cent of their timetable. Not surprisingly, the vision of spending 80 per cent of their time in mainstream classes in a school accommodating over 1,600 students and hundreds of staff is very daunting and only deepens any existing insecurities resulting from language delay caused by deafness. As well as using students' time in the Deaf Support Centre to catch up on other school work, we prefer to present them with an enjoyable task, allowing them to produce quality work they, or anybody, would be proud of. The sense of empowerment and achievement that comes from this approach is crucial to a positive and confident identity as both a learner and a Deaf person.

to the task; engaged and enthusiastic, he started typing his story without prompting. It wasn't only the process of typing that allowed him to correct his mistakes and make his work look neat and perfect that motivated him, but also the idea of emailing his work to the teacher and waiting for a response.

The use of ICT has transformed a conventional written assignment into an exchange of information with the teacher on equal terms. Since then, Alex has been allowed to use different programs in Learning Support lessons to produce his work. He has tried Comic Life and Pages alongside filming and subtitling, together with posting examples of his work onto a group blog (see Figure 7.2). Web-based learning and blogging has also been an exciting way of involving parents in their children's work and sharing their learning with them, facilitating further learning at home and providing an important platform for contact and discussion.

Such approaches have helped compensate for the gap that had opened up between Alex's topic knowledge and his ability to express himself with written language prior to transition, supporting a more confident start to his secondary school career. It has also alerted teachers to the needs of such students when they arrive and provided a link between home and school, which will be essential for continued success.

Key learning points

Students with additional difficulties such as deafness/hearing impairment often develop a gap between their topic knowledge and ability to express this in written form. Such students can become acutely aware of their shortcomings in this way, especially when compared to hearing peers. ICT can be creatively employed to allow students to express their knowledge in their 'first' language (BSL) and thus develop greater confidence in their own ability and their identity as learners.

The use of technology in the Deaf Support Centre facilitates exciting learning where students are engaged, challenged and stimulated, not only by the finished product, but also by the process of making it. It also teaches them to take responsibility for the equipment they handle and their own work, both fundamental to successful long-term learning.

A key feature of the students' learning during the project has been the extent to which they develop greater independence and enthusiasm for taking responsibility for their own decisions. A group of students who had become accustomed to looking outside of themselves for support are now showing signs of willingness to find their own way of coping with the significant challenges they face.

EDITOR'S COMMENTS

As ICT and new media become more widespread and accessible, the potential benefits of using technology to support the needs of a variety of learners raise important implications for everyday teaching and learning. Schools may find it helpful to consider how alternative forms of communication, aided by technology, can be utilised in mainstream as well as special education contexts. This will have some implications for staff training, so it may also be helpful to consider how staff can be supported in acquiring and sharing the necessary skills to develop these approaches. Read on to see how Thomas Tallis have begun to grapple with these challenges. . .

What next?

As we became aware of the learning gains made possible by the approaches that we had attempted at Thomas Tallis, we started to consider how we might share some of this good practice with other schools with support centres and their students. To fund this activity we made a bid to the Greenwich Deaf Advisory Service with the following ambitions:

- To create a pathway from early years to post-16 education to enable students and staff to develop their use of new media to support learning.
- To use new media to develop resources and teaching to make the curriculum more accessible for Deaf students.
- To develop and share expertise about new media between different support bases in the Deaf Advisory Service.
- To allow access to technologies that develop student independence, communication skills and enhance student self-esteem.
- To record and share learning and resources more effectively among students, parents, teachers and community groups.

The plan was for the Deaf Support Centre at Thomas Tallis to act as a hub for the development of the use of new technologies and new media and for an individual within the primary schools and in post-16 colleges that had Deaf students and support bases to work alongside us to develop and apply their skills. Individuals from the different support centres would attend a day's training each term and the person leading the project would make a termly visit to the different centres. Once colleagues in these centres felt that they had achieved a level of competence and confidence through their own work with students they would then seek to extend the programme to other colleagues within their centre.

The scheme is now in its second year and has thrown up some interesting challenges and directed all of us towards some potential solutions, which we continue to debate – how we support staff with less experience of ICT being an example issue. In relation to this, a project between Thomas Tallis School and local primary schools has sought to develop competence with new technologies in the primary sector. Rather than the day-to-day engagement being led by a teaching member of staff, the project is led by a media technician who spends one day a week in the schools working on a project that is developed from the school's existing curriculum. These termly projects allow for staff to accelerate their learning and confidence, generating greater momentum for the use of new technologies. They also leave an important legacy for how such technologies might be employed more widely across the curriculum. We are also seeking ways of employing similar projects and methods to allow for those Deaf centres that require more support to receive it.

'Life & Deaf II – the movie' is also scheduled for release in 2012 . . .

Resources

Books

Passy, J. (2010) *Cued Articulation – Consonants and Vowels*, Melbourne, Australia: Australian Council for Educational Research. This is a good book if you would like to know more about cued articulation, as referred to in the chapter. See also this YouTube video featuring Jane Passy: http://www.youtube.com/watch?v=YBJ9-SBe2eI

Sparrowhawk, A. and Heald, Y. (2007) *How to Use ICT to Support Children with Special Educational Needs*, Cambridge: LDA. This book is for practitioners and gives a good overview about how ICT can be used to support students with special needs in general.

Websites:

Life & Deaf website: http://www.lifeanddeaf.co.uk
Creative Tallis blog: http://creativetallis.blogspot.com
Creative Tallis: http://www.creativetallis.com
Richard's blog: http://richardachiampong.weebly.com/
Tallis Lab blog: http://tallislab.tumblr.com
Tallis Lab website: http://www.tallislab.com

Web 2.0 Tools

Tumblr (http://www.tumblr.com): a user-friendly blogging platform with lots of exciting and well-designed templates.

Weebly (http://www.weebly.com): build your own website easily and for free with this online web design service.

Xtranormal (http://www.xtranormal.com): easily create text to speech animated movies in minutes.

Voki (http://www.voki.com): create an animated talking avatar for your blog or website.

Software:

iMovie 09
Final Cut Express

CPD ACTIVITY

As a staff discuss one of these case studies and compare the account to a pupil from your own school, whose additional needs prevent him/her from demonstrating what he/she learned. Discuss what alternative forms of support and assessment are available, and what would be the implications of offering such a student an opportunity to choose how they showed what they had learned.

Chapter 8

Creative approaches to promoting voice

Mary Kirby and David Stewart, Oak Field Special School (formerly Shepherd Special School), Nottingham

Editor's introduction

This chapter describes i) the need to equip students with profound, multiple and/or severe learning difficulties with the communicational tools to express their views on matters affecting their health and education, ii) how pupil consultation and research projects have informed and enhanced curriculum resources, and iii) how student voice projects have extended beyond the school building to raise awareness and challenge stereotypes within their local, national and international communities.

> ### HOW TO USE THIS CHAPTER
>
> This chapter focuses on creative approaches to developing pupil voice at two levels, within and beyond the school. It will be relevant to any professional grappling with how to promote pupil voice work with pupils with special needs and/or those students who need a great deal of support in expressing their views.

The school context

Oak Field School and Sports College, an amalgamation of two successful special schools (Shepherd and Aspley Wood Schools), began life in September 2009 and moved to its brand new purpose-built site in November of the same year. The work referred to in this chapter began at Shepherd Special School and has been taken into the new school. For ease of reference, we will refer to the projects under the new school name, Oak Field.

Oak Field now caters for 140 pupils aged 3–19 with profound and multiple learning difficulties (PMLD), severe learning disabilities (SLD), physical disabilities (PD) and other pupils with complex needs. For students with PMLD their main difficulties may include a physical disability, a sensory impairment and/or a possible severe medical condition. Students with SLD often have acute global development delay and cognitive or intellectual impairment posing significant difficulties for such pupils to follow a curriculum without substantial help and support. Many students will have a number of these conditions.

The challenge

Figure 8.1 Levels of voice – speech and language therapists at Oak Field

Level 1 – voice communicating basic needs and wants via advocacy
Level 2 – voice communicating basic needs and wants
Level 3 – voice within relationships
Level 4 – voice within the school
Level 5 – voice beyond the school

It was only in the 1970s that children in the UK with the most severe learning difficulties were first considered to be the responsibility of the education system as well as the National Health Service. Significant strides have taken place since and current education policy advocates inclusive approaches to education and endorses the UN Convention on the Rights of the Child, which encourages all schools to consult their pupils and involve them where possible in decision-making processes, particularly concerning issues affecting them directly.

However, students with severe learning difficulties encounter significant intellectual and communicational obstacles when discussing their learning, personal decisions and life choices. Therefore, our challenge has been: how do we encourage young people to express their voice on important issues affecting them?

When thinking about voice amongst students with extreme difficulties it is helpful to discuss the different levels at which a pupil may be able to express their views (see Figure 8.1).

Whereas all these levels are important, we also wanted to challenge ourselves to help students move from expressing their views about basic needs to important messages about their experiences in the wider community, where possible. Hence this chapter is about voice within and beyond the school. We will report several projects where students have sought to change attitudes, and raise consciousness in their community as well as make meaningful relationships with others. We regard this as important because our duty to our students extends beyond equipping students with communication skills. It also includes educating communities about disability so our students encounter less prejudice when they express themselves beyond the school boundary. Hence our second challenge concerns: how do we encourage our students to become active members of their own school and wider community?

This chapter will focus on some of the communication work undertaken with our 16–18-year-old students. It will show how students can contribute to valuable user group research in order to enrich their learning experiences as well as how they can acquire life skills for managing their own decisions and relationships. Our greatest success has been student-led research that has given some of our students the opportunity, skills and confidence to take part in national and international conferences.

Our timeline

1990	'Living Your Life' first written
2000	Staff and students present at a conference in Seattle
2002	Staff and students present at a conference in Dublin
2002	Started working with Creative Partnerships

2003	'Living Your Life' 2nd edition developed
	'Musical Futures' Project begins
2004	'Listen to Us' Project
	Staff and students present at a conference in Maastricht
2006	'Bodyworks' resource developed
2008	Staff and students present at ISAID conference in South Africa
Jun 2009	Students present at 'Moving Forwards' Conference
Nov 2009	Shepherd School join with Aspley Wood to form Oak Field School and move to a new purpose-built school
Jan 2010	School cafe opens to the public
Apr 2011	'Living Your Life' – 3rd edition published

Issues that challenge pupil voice in special education

Alongside the national and international impetus to promote pupil voice, our school has always placed a great emphasis on championing our students' views both in school and in their local, national and international communities. We recognise the challenge that pupils with additional needs face in establishing their voice, the importance of being listened to and also that their wishes are acted upon in light of their requests or suggestions.

Before we discuss some of our projects, it is helpful to consider the different ways in which a pupil with learning difficulties communicates. Figure 8.2 lists a selection of these.

For some children, expressing voice using these resources still remains a challenge, even in a supportive environment and in these cases it is also important to consider the role of advocacy. Students with special needs are entitled to be in control of their own lives as much as possible, so the role of an advocate is to help students express their needs and wishes effectively. This means that our staff need to develop trusting relationships and sophisticated approaches to interpreting, understanding and representing pupils' views.

Whether a young person's communication flourishes or not can be highly influenced by a supporter's expectations. Staff need to be equipped with the skills to recognise a pupil's attempt to communicate and to understand that every student can make a contribution. If staff have low expectations then the pupil voice will be more difficult to discern. For

Figure 8.2 Ways of communicating without speech

- Body language
- Facial expression
- Eye pointing
- Use of objects of reference to signal events or to make choices
- Communication aids
- Augmentative and alternative communication aids (devices programmed specifically for each student)
- Photographs, pictures and symbols
- Print
- Signing
- ICT
- Sounds and spoken word
- Facilitated communication (a process where the facilitator supports the hand or arm of a communicatively impaired individual when using a keyboard or other devices)

Figure 8.3 Hart's ladder of participation

DEGREES OF PARTICIPATION	8. Child-initiated, shared decision with adults
	7. Child-initiated and directed.
	6. Adult-initiated, shared decisions with children
	5. Consulted but informed
	4. Assigned but informed
NON PARTICIPATION	3. Tokenism
	2. Decoration
	1. Manipulation

students with less severe intellectual and communicational challenges at our school, there is no reason why pupil voice projects cannot be more ambitious.

When considering how best to support student voice, it is important to consider the level of voice we are trying to encourage and the degree of participation afforded the child. We have found the ladder of pupil participation by Roger Hart (see Figure 8.3 and resource list) helpful as it highlights the degree of a pupil's real participation with an activity. Hart designed the ladder to acknowledge that students with a range of additional and diverse needs can access it at any point and still be recognised for their valid participation. The ladder shows eight stages of participation separated by degrees of adult support. Hart draws particular attention to the shortcomings of manipulation, decoration and tokenism, suggesting these fall short of real participation as the support person for the child retains too much control.

As an illustration, wheeling a young person onto a performance stage, whilst making no contribution, would not count as participation, it would be decoration. This is particularly important for the work at Oak Field. Like other special and mainstream settings, we are constantly challenged to provide meaningful experiences of participation where possible as it is very easy for adults to take too much control under the guise of pupil advocacy, voice and empowerment.

Tokenism can be extremely prevalent with regards to students with learning difficulties. One of the challenges that we face in special education is that we seek to sustain and make opportunities valuable and meaningful to all the students involved. We hope that some of the projects shared in this chapter serve as good examples.

Voices and choices

Our post-16 students are placed in the perilous position of having to decide which options to take after leaving school. They usually have a wide range of communication abilities and some may present challenging behaviour when out in the community, out of routine, or not engaged with an activity. A further challenge is that many of our post-16 students join us at this stage of their education and are thus less familiar with the organisational structures and communicational approaches of our school. We became acutely aware of the need to support all these students in finding communication strategies to enable them to express their voices in lessons, school and community based activities and also at their leavers' reviews. We were also aware of the need to remain flexible to a diversity of need within the group.

One challenge our post-16 group encountered was that the communication between pupils often ceased when they came into formal classroom settings. Yet, when the students were undertaking activities in the community, taking part in physical education and fitness options, they communicated with peers and staff more freely and effectively. Having worked with Creative Partnerships and other outside arts agencies in the past, we realised the potential creativity may play in encouraging these students to relax and express their voice.

We initially chose music as a stimulus and medium for sessions about communication. The group were motivated by pop music idols and were familiar with songs popular at the time. This type of work was inspired by the Musical Futures initiatives in mainstream settings (see resource list), which allows pupils to take a lead in steering their own learning through music. The class formed a rock band, aided by sheet music that had been adapted to show symbols, easy to handle instruments, lights, smoke and lots of enthusiasm! Members of staff also joined the band to model effective communication skills.

These sessions had tight but seemingly informal structures, starting with a physical and voice warm up. This was teacher led at first but soon the students began to take ownership of the process. Students were given band names and chose aliases through watching video clips of popular artists. We felt an alternative persona might empower students, allowing them to pretend to be a new person with a different voice.

Students formed small working groups, some singing, some rapping, some backing or musically accompanying the group. The sessions ran for a term and songs varied every three weeks, each decided by students. By running the same song for three weeks students developed their confidence and communication skills and felt they had ownership of the sessions. The session provided the students with opportunities and reasons to communicate in a structured and safe environment. Having undertaken some work with students to develop their capacity and confidence to express their voice it became important to support them in applying these skills to real-life contexts and issues as for these students the most pressing concern was the choices of further education, or alternative pathways, they were about to make.

We started by doing some work around key and relevant vocabulary. This exercise was informed by the group making trips to each day-centre/college offering options to our students and collecting pictorial records of these visits. We then ran a session modelling how to express opinions about places from a particular perspective. Key phrases such as 'I liked. . . .' and 'It would be better if . . .' were emphasised alongside the use of cue cards, symbols and photos.

By informing the students about the choices on the horizon and modelling decision-making skills, the students were able to create individual leavers' profiles to support them in their leavers' presentations, assisting them to make some of the most important decisions of their adult lives in a more informed manner. Clearly, there is a very delicate balance to be struck between support, guidance and influence. As trustworthiness and professional judgement are so important, it is wise for schools to think about how to ensure these attributes are responsibly employed. At Oak Field, we do this through a de-briefing exercise with colleagues acting as critical friends.

Voices and personal relationships

Another pressing area in which students need to be able to express themselves very clearly and assertively is in adult personal relationships. All of our students will encounter a discrepancy between how ready their bodies and how ready their minds are for sexual relationships, which makes them particularly vulnerable. Personal Health and Social Education (PSHE) lessons are instrumental to the lives of the young people at Oak Field School for this reason. Hence, they need to be given the social and communicational tools to lead happy, safe and fulfilled lives.

During PSHE lessons many strategies are employed to encourage and nurture student voice. Some of these are shown in Figure 8.4.

Students have benefited greatly from two particular programmes of study in PSHE; these are: 'Body works' (a PSHE resource developed to support PMLD students' understanding of their bodies – see resource list) and 'Living Your Life' (a similar resource about leading an independent adult life and managing relationships for SLD students – also see resource list). As well as an example of learning how to express voice in personal relationships, the development of 'Living Your Life' is also an excellent example of how students have been engaged in the research and development of an educational resource to benefit others.

With appropriate support and training, students demonstrated that they had particular views and ideas on both their bodies and relationships, which they were keen to share in dialogue. A user group was formed to research the development of these resources and met on a monthly basis. Example sessions from the resource were trialled and students made suggestions for improvements, giving their feedback via photos, symbols or communication aids. This user-group helped to make 'Living Your Life' a very powerful resource for other young people with special needs.

One particular example of how the students informed the process was through a discussion around the pictures/visual aids we use to support the pack. The students looked at the line drawings depicting the stages of a relationship. One of the members of the group made vocalisations and pointed to his bag. An advocate gave him the bag and he found his phone. He turned on his mobile phone and showed the group this video he'd been sent of a song and cartoon images of a relationship. The graphics and the song were helpful to the student and highlighted that we needed to think beyond paper resources to develop computer programs and real characters to support the 'Living Your Life' resource (see Figure 8.5).

Figure 8.4 Strategies for encouraging voice in PSHE lessons

Strategy:	Reason:
Gender specific groups	To encourage open discussion around sensitive issues.
Team teaching sessions	To allow one teacher to lead and the other to become skilled at facilitating student responses.
Set routines and structures to start and finish	To provide students with a set routine that encourages pupil participation and gives students ownership of the session.
Using real life objects/ symbols and photographs (visual aids)	To support students' communication and understanding of the topic.
Using a variety of drama techniques such as role play and hot seating	To model people's behaviour effectively. To provide students with a stimulus to talk about.
Keeping an informal layout to the room i.e. a circle of chairs	To encourage discussion, openness and turn taking in the group.

PUBLIC TOILETS
James and William are shopping in town.
They need to use the toilet.
In the toilets, there are urinals and
cubicles. They must choose.
William uses the cubicle.
He locks the door.
He takes his trousers down
and sits on the toilet.
When he has finished,
he uses the toilet paper and
wipes his bottom carefully.
He pulls up and
fastens his trousers.
William washes and
dries his hands

Figure 8.5 Image of a page from 'Living Your Life'

Voice and friendships

One of the concerns for us as a school is that we encourage friendship groups and activities in the safe school environment but then there are limited opportunities for friendships to grow outside the school and later on in life. To highlight this problem, one PSHE class for 16–19-year-olds explored the activities they might do with a friend. We posed the question, 'what would you like to do with a friend outside of school?' The students were encouraged to collate objects, symbols and words that were related to things friends might do together. Their collection included a Play Station 3, dinner plates, pub pictures, a cinema timetable and so on and there was excitement about these ideas.

However, the mood changed when we asked, 'what do you do with *your* friends outside of school?' One student talked about having a friend around for tea only once a term. Most pointed to symbols of link workers (who are paid to be with them) and talked fondly about times with them but then explained that they had little or no time outside of school with friends.

It was apparent that many of our students only have very few friends out of school and few opportunities to engage in activities popular with other teenagers. This also meant they had little opportunity to practice communication with their peers as well as a lack of common experiences to talk about at school. The issue of friendships and how pupils develop a voice that enables them to create opportunities for themselves to develop and maintain friendships has now become a significant feature of work at our school.

The Quality Network Review (see resource list), which involved members of staff from Oak Field in its development, is an audit designed to check the quality of life for children and young people with learning disabilities in ten key areas:

- making everyday choices
- making important decisions
- being treated with respect
- taking part in everyday activities
- having friendships and relationships
- being healthy
- being safe from bullying and abuse
- having the chance to work
- being part of the local community
- having the views of their families heard.

When undertaken with one of our PSHE classes for 16–18-year-olds in 2004, the review highlighted that none of the nine young people surveyed had friends and relationships outside school 'a lot of the time', seven young people 'sometimes' had friends and relationships and two 'never' had friends and relationships. The review identified that students with SLD needed many more opportunities in the community and far greater support to access a comparable level of social resources as their peers.

To respond to these needs, we offer regular opportunities in school to support pupil voice in their friendships. These include:

- a weekly timetable slot for friendship times
- friendship groups for younger pupils
- leisure options for older students, where they can choose who they would like to be with and what they would like to do
- after-hours clubs: Sports Club, Arts Plus, 'Let's Get Cooking' and the Duke of Edinburgh Award
- evening theatre visits
- drama groups
- residential excursions both during school time and weekends
- holidays for current and former students.

These are essential aspects of extended provision because for students with learning difficulties their school is a hub for social experience, and sometimes so for many years after leaving school.

Tailored support around transition into adulthood continues to be part of the school's continuing development plan. The new school, as part of the 'Building Schools for the Future' programme, has a fully-equipped flat to offer pupils experiences to learn independent living skills with appropriate levels of support (see Figure 8.6).

Voice and the wider world

Oak Field has tried to nurture students' communication abilities both in school and beyond. By the time our students leave, they are equipped with a repertoire of skills and/or means

Figure 8.6 The school-based apartment

to communicate. Where relevant these are transferred to other settings, as well as the home, to support smooth transitions.

We have run user and student research groups for many years in order to inform school decision-making processes with the views of students. The outcome of one such research group, given the task to research things about school life, was both unexpected and profound. Their conclusion was that school was actually a haven for them and that it was in the wider community they encountered problems, so their work led to awareness raising of disability in neighbouring schools.

This work has continued to develop in recent years. 'Listen to Us' (see resource list) was a successful project bringing together young people with disabilities from mainstream and special schools to develop a teaching resource for schools about the lives of those with disabilities. The group was joined by two young people without disabilities. Feedback from those who have read about living with a disability have expressed their shock at these accounts. The voice of young people with disabilities has thus given readers of this resource greater insight and understanding of what the lives of the young people with disabilities are really like.

We also receive regular invitations to discuss our work and contribute to conferences locally, nationally and internationally. When this occurs, we see this as an opportunity to invite our students to present at these events, believing fully that it should be the learners with special needs talking about the reality of their lives and not just people speaking on their behalf. By allowing the students to present at the conferences, the young people are also challenging stereotypes of learning disabilities

As an illustration, we attended a conference in 2009, organised by the Specialist Schools and Academies Trust. The conference focus was on 'Moving Forward' and people from all over the country were invited to listen to keynote speakers around the new initiatives and provision available to learners with special needs. Staff and students were invited to lead a keynote presentation about the central theme, so we asked five former students aged 18, 20, 28, 31 and 35 to present at the conference. The ages were significant because each student would be able to highlight the challenges and successes they encountered at different stages in their adult lives.

Students were supported to talk about their experiences of school, transition and life experiences, aided by cue cards, symbols and photographs. Each student worked on creating an individualised resource to support them with their talk, as shown in Figure 8.7.

Presenting to 200 people requires a huge amount of knowledge and confidence. A great deal of preparatory work was undertaken so each presenter was equipped with a range of skills:

- knowing when to talk and when to listen
- how to share the forum with others
- responding to unknown questions
- turn taking
- learning appropriate vocabulary
- developing coping strategies for difficult points in the presentation.

The conference contribution was extremely well received as the students' voices were powerful and stirring, hopefully also raising people's expectations of what students with SLD can achieve with appropriate support.

Figure 8.7 An ex-pupil's resource card to support their conference presentation

Key learning points

School culture and leadership issues

Whether pupils are given the opportunity to develop a voice will depend largely on a number of supportive cultural factors, characterised by:

- openness
- high expectations and pupil empowerment
- an environment that makes pupils feel valued and secure
- demonstrating to pupils they are listened to and what they have to say has worth
- dedicated curriculum time and extended provision to encourage friendship, socialisation and the development of communication skills
- a commitment to advocacy
- creative staff, who are patient and skilled in various forms of communication
- family support and plans for transition.

A pertinent issues for managers and leaders is the need to give due consideration to what is done when pupil voice is expressed. What will be the response? Whilst our school will always try and accommodate requests from pupils, there needs to be mature debate that whilst someone may express a view or an opinion, it may be challenged or not acted upon for a wide range of reasons. This needs to be explained clearly at the onset of a project. Far better to be upfront than to pretend that whatever a pupil says will be acted upon and then later do nothing.

Interpreting student voice and developing user groups

When developing pupil voice it is essential to support their basic enabling skills (such as the communication of their immediate needs and wishes) and we have found processes of observation and analysis central to the development of features of their personalised communication programme (i.e. how these needs and wishes are translated via specific strategies that may be unique to them). Given the severity and complexity of the needs of some of our students, additional training for staff is essential in a range of communicational approaches. All staff also need to become acquainted with the role and demands of being an advocate as a means to supporting meaningful communication.

With appropriate levels of expectations, a 'can do' school culture and staff commitment in place, we have enjoyed great success enabling student voice through experiences both in school and beyond. User groups have regularly been formed to review resources, curriculum innovation and student research groups work with both our local universities on various projects. Such opportunities, alongside those to present at conferences, have meant that many of our students have become advocates for their peers with learning disabilities at national and international levels.

When instigating user or student research groups for students with special needs, we have found the following tips critical to their success.

OAK FIELD'S TOP TEN TIPS

(for establishing student research or user groups)

1 Establish protocols with researchers on the way they work with students. Make it clear that there must be an end benefit to the students.
2 If the research is financed through a grant, make sure sufficient funds have been allocated to support such a group – for refreshments, transport and facilitator.
3 The group must have clear ground rules. Important to have a voice but equally important to listen to others.
4 If the project is time limited – make this clear and plan exit strategy so that students have time to understand this.
5 Ensure that there is a facilitator to support students and prepare for the meetings with researchers.
6 Make sure that meetings of the group are fairly regular; say once a month, so that students have a sense of routine.
7 Establish whether the students are there as representatives of others or giving opinions as individuals. If the former they may need support in how they gather the views of others.
8 Each meeting can also be an opportunity for socialisation so make sure time is given for refreshment and greeting. Meetings held out of school time are always popular. Two and a half to three hours is often about the right length of time to allow for work and pleasure.
9 The use of storyboarding and graphics to record meetings is helpful as they allow for a pictorial record, which acts as an aide memoir for subsequent meetings.
10 Decide how you will bring new members to the groups and think carefully and sensitively about those who may need to move on. Such groups can quickly provide a social setting for students, which they do not want to leave.

What next?

Staff at Oak Field School continue to develop new PSHE programmes of study to meet a diversity of students' needs. The development of such resources includes opportunities for pupil consultation and less experienced staff to receive training to support this process.

User groups continue to be instrumental, students lead on projects underpinning new programmes and ideas alongside staff from the school, local universities and other settings. We realise the importance of ensuring as many students as possible have the opportunity to contribute to these projects and we work hard to make this possible. Students are fully supported in this process by staff with a good knowledge and understanding of the communication strategies they prefer alongside advocacy training.

As an illustration, 'Living Your Life' was reviewed by a new user group, supported by staff in school and its professional partners, who are skilled in advocating for students. The new edition was published in 2011.

Pupil voice in the community remains a key focus for Oak Field School and various user groups are currently running. The school is working hard at developing work experience programmes for our post-16 students in the community. Examples of current opportunities include placement in local hairdressers, transport offices and charity shops. These opportunities provide the students with hands-on, real life communication with people in the local community as well as raising people's awareness and challenging stereotypes of learning disability in the community.

The new school also boasts a cafe, run by our older students and supporting staff (see Figure 8.8). Training is currently in process and it is hoped that the cafe will be open to the public, giving pupils further opportunity to develop communication skills whilst delivering a service to members of their local community. Other plans include using the flat in school to host friendship evenings where pupils can have supported friendship time in safe and supported conditions. We are also continuing to develop meaningful projects with local mainstream primary and secondary schools to enhance pupil voice, develop inclusive attitudes to disability and raise expectations concerning what students with SLD can do in the wider community.

Resources

Hart, R. (1997) *Children's Participation: The Theory and Practice of Involving Young Citizens in Community Development and Environmental Care*, New York: UNICEF. An interesting book to read if you would like to know more about Hart's ladder of participation, as cited in the chapter.

Figure 8.8 The school cafe

PSHE

Bodyworks – PSHE resource for students with PMLD
Listen to US – A citizenship education resource for young people with special needs.
Living Your Life – PSHE resource for students with SLD
Available from – Oak Field School, Wigman Road, Nottingham NG8 3HW, UK. Tel:+44 (0)115 0153264; email: admin@oakfield.nottingham.sch.uk

Websites

http://www.musicalfutures.org/ Musical Futures is an innovative initiative that supports new approaches to the teaching and learning of *music* in and out of the classroom.
http://www.bild.org.uk/tqn/ For information about the Quality Network Review, which can be used as an audit of the quality of life for young people with disabilities.
http://www.whatkidscando.org/ 'What kids can do' is a website promoting perceptions of young people as valued resources, not problems, and advocating learning that engages students as knowledge creators and a means for bringing youth voices to policy debates about school, society, and world affairs.

CPD ACTIVITY

Start by working in small groups to discuss the following.

Discussion point 1

Consider who has the least capacity to express their voice in your school and why. Record your key points on flip chart paper and share with members of the team.

Discussion point 2

Consider an activity that such a student finds challenging. Complete the following table, thinking about how existing strategies are employed at different levels to engage their voice (column 2). Then highlight these according to Hart's ladder of participation, using one colour for 'tokenism' for example. Then discuss the pattern. Where strategies are deemed manipulative, decorative or tokenistic, try and identify potential strategies that offer fuller participation (column 3).

Strategy	Current strategies	Potential strategies
Layout of the room		
Language used in class		
Objects/pictorial support		
Advocate		
Activities		
Expectations		
Other		

Discussion point 3

Highlight strategies from column 3 that could be identified as priorities for the school and discuss what would be involved in their implementation.

Index